6-5-75

Economies of the World

EDITED BY

NITA WATTS

TRENTINO-ADIGE
FRIULI-VENEZIA GIULIA
VALLE D'AOSTA
LOMBARDY
Milan
Brescia
VENEZIA
Verona
Trieste
Turin
PIEDMONT
Venice
Padua
Parma
EMILIA ROMAGNA
Modena
Bologna
Ravenna
LIGURIA
Genoa
ADRIATIC SEA
Florence
Leghorn
TUSCANY
LIGURIAN SEA
MARCHE
UMBRIA
Pescara
ABRUZZI AND MOLISE
LATIUM
Rome
MT. GARGANO
Foggia
CAMPANIA
Naples
Bari
APULIA
Porto Torres
Salerno
BASILICATA
Potenza
(LUCANIA)
Brindisi
Taranto
SARDINIA
TYRRHENIAN SEA
IONIAN SEA
Cagliari
CALABRIA
Crotone
SILA
Messina
Palermo
Reggio di Calabria
SICILY
Catania
Siracusa
Gela
Ragusa
Border between Centre – North and Mezzogiorno
0 50 100 150km

Italy

Italy:

DEVELOPMENT AND CRISIS IN THE POST-WAR ECONOMY

BY

GISELE PODBIELSKI

CLARENDON PRESS · OXFORD

1974

Oxford University Press, Ely House, London W.1

GLASGOW NEW YORK TORONTO MELBOURNE WELLINGTON
CAPE TOWN IBADAN NAIROBI DAR ES SALAAM LUSAKA ADDIS ABABA
DELHI BOMBAY CALCUTTA MADRAS KARACHI LAHORE DACCA
KUALA LUMPUR SINGAPORE HONG KONG TOKYO

CASEBOUND ISBN 0 19 877032 4
PAPERBACK ISBN 0 19 877033 2

PRINTED IN GREAT BRITAIN BY
RICHARD CLAY (THE CHAUCER PRESS) LTD,
BUNGAY, SUFFOLK

EDITORIAL PREFACE

Economies of the World is designed as a series for readers in universities, business, and government, and provides brief reviews of economic developments during the last 20–25 years in each of a number of countries. The countries selected for study are either of obvious importance in the world economy or interesting because of particular features of their economic structure or recent history, or because their experience throws light on more widespread problems of economic development.

Each volume contains a summary description of the pace and pattern of economic growth in the period covered; and it outlines the main economic problems confronting government in the country, the objectives of economic policy, and the chosen means of economic management. But each author then focuses attention on those aspects of the country's development which he considers most deserving of more detailed examination. The volumes do not attempt to provide comprehensive descriptions and analyses, but they give enough statistical data to support the author's conclusions and a bibliography to suggest further reading.

The series is intended for those interested in problems of

NOTE

For reasons beyond the publisher's control, the publication of this book has been delayed by six months. The time-lag between the events described in the concluding chapter and current developments in the Italian economy is therefore unusually long. Moreover the economic—and political—situation of the country has deteriorated dramatically in the first half of 1974. But, while the factual description in Chapter 10 is partly out of date, the analysis of the factors which underlie the protracted economic difficulties of recent years and culminated in the unprecedentedly severe 1974 crisis remains valid.

July 1974

CONTENTS

LIST OF FIGURES

NOTE

Throughout this work, the term 'billion' denotes 'a thousand millions', rather than 'a million millions'.

I gratefully acknowledge the permission of O.E.C.D. and the Brookings Institution to reproduce figures and tables on pages 19, 109, 123 and 155. Other tabular or diagrammatic materials have been constructed on the basis of data from the sources noted in the underlines.

LIST OF TABLES

INTRODUCTION

THIS study on the post-war Italian economy does not claim to offer any completely new findings or to arrive at startling conclusions. Many of the data and the arguments could be found somewhere in the many excellent reports already published in Italy and abroad. But most of these studies cover either more limited periods of time or deal only with particular aspects of the Italian experience. The aim of this volume is first to present a concise general review of Italian economic development in the whole of the post-war period and, against this background, to highlight some aspects of the problems both of short-term management of the economy and of securing necessary structural changes.

I have drawn upon a wide range of sources of information, many available only in Italian, and have attempted to present sufficiently comprehensive statistical evidence for my descriptions and arguments.

It is impossible to enumerate all the persons who were helpful to me in the collection of material and in answering my questions. But I wish to express my warm thanks to Professor Augusto Graziani who has found time to elucidate some questions in writing; to Dr. Giorgio Ruffolo who gave me his views on some major issues in a particularly difficult phase of his work; to Dr. Almerina Ipsevich of ISCO (Institute for Conjuncture) for helping me to understand some of the short-term problems; to Professor Paolo Sylos-Labini and Professor Luigi Spaventa for covering a great many questions in long interviews and for letting me have some new studies; to Professor Sergio Steve for an informative discussion of budgetary policy; to Dr. Franco Archibugi for his survey of planning problems; and to Dr. Carlo Tresoldi and a number of his colleagues at the Bank of Italy. Dr. Tresoldi, in particular, gave me a great deal of his time in providing explanations of some of the finer points of the

Bank of Italy Annual Reports and was also invaluable to me in supplying me with some background statistics.

I also wish to express my gratitude to my former colleague at the United Nations Economic Commission for Europe in Geneva, Dr. Carlo Zacchia, for his lucid views on Italian economic developments and to members of the research staff of the O.E.C.D. for sending me statistical and analytical material of great interest.

Most especially, my gratitude must go to my old friend and colleague at the E.C.E., Nita Watts, who has greatly improved my book. She has pointed out flaws in the structure and the argument of my first draft and has made invaluable suggestions about the style of presentation.

With all the help that I have received, mistakes may seem unforgivable; they doubtless exist and are my own.

The Italian economy experienced a process of rapid and apparently smooth growth and transformation in the 1950s. In the 1960s and early 1970s it was twice faced with the problem—familiar also to other western European countries—of reconciling growth with internal and external stability. Despite progress, the Italian economy is today still substantially lagging behind other advanced industrial countries with respect to such indicators of economic development as gross national product per head, the share of industry in gross domestic product, the level of *per capita* private consumption, and the share of national income devoted to investment in machinery and equipment.

But the fundamental difference between Italy and the rest of industrial Europe and North America lies in the fact that Italy has been, and still is, confronted with structural imbalances and distortions of a magnitude generally unknown to other advanced industrial economies. These manifest themselves in the disparities between technologically progressive, competitive, export-oriented and large-scale industries, on the one hand, and backward, inefficient, traditional industrial and service sectors dominated by small and medium-sized enterprises on the other; between a rapid growth of private consumption and a highly inadequate level and slow advance of collective consumption; between shortages of skilled workers in some areas and the persistence of a large-scale under-utilization of labour resources in others; between excessive urbanization and congestion and the abandonment of rural regions.

All these aspects of an economic and social 'dualism' appear in even sharper contrast in the development gap between the Centre–North and the South of the country. Added to these are differences in levels of education and training, in political and social outlook and in behaviour patterns.

The structural disequilibria of the Italian economy have been accentuated, rather than mitigated, by a top-heavy public administration run by opposing political factions and group interests and weakened in its decision-making by political instability. There has been a pervasive resistance to change and reform, stemming from a fear that these might limit the exercise of arbitrary power and might damage vested interests; and even when legal decisions for reform have been taken, numerous institutional and procedural obstacles have prevented or delayed their implementation.

The failure of the authorities to get overdue structural changes under way, and thus to provide a sounder basis for a successful operation of both the public and the private sector and to promote the improvement of the social conditions of the working population, has deepened the long-standing public mistrust of government and the public administration. It has more recently led to recurrent outbursts of social unrest and sometimes violence.

It is hardly possible to explain all these phenomena in economic terms alone. This is not the place to attempt to supply a full historical, political, and sociological explanation of the present difficulties confronting the Italian economy. But some aspects of Italy's past cannot be wholly overlooked in this context.

Italy has remained less unified than other developed countries; and, in the course of a long history, has failed to make its society more homogeneous. While this failure has had as a by-product a remarkable burst of individual genius, economically the historical lack of unity on the peninsula has been, and remains, a burden.

The basic premiss for disunity was geographical. Italy's rugged terrain permitted and even encouraged the creation of small states whose independence of one another—if not of foreign powers—lasted well into the last century. Social and economic unification was slowed down even within most of these states by mountain barriers and by the lack of navigable rivers; and until 1860, out of a total of 1,848 villages in the Kingdom of Naples, 1,621 had no roads whatsoever communicating with other settlements.

Another geographic characteristic is the shape and position of the country. The distance from Turin to Palermo is more than a thousand miles; and the different rates and patterns of development of the North and the South are partly due to this distance. If the Mediterranean had remained the centre of civilization, Sicily and Calabria and not Piedmont and Lombardy might today be Italy's most advanced regions. As it was, the more rapid evolution of the North owes much to its proximity to European centres of progress which provided a stimulus lacking in the South.

The history played out on this stage has had peculiar features which, like Italy's geography, have prevented the Italian people from building a society and state resembling those of other European nations.

Even the two great organizational feats of antiquity have hampered unification. Both the Roman Empire and the Roman Church have encouraged literate Italians to take a cosmopolitan rather than a national view of their political destiny. Visions of empire, stimulated by a rhetoric which did not die until after the Second World War, often diverted an otherwise realistic people from knitting together their own society. The universalism of the real heir to the Roman Empire—the Catholic Church—also constituted a hindrance to unity. As Machiavelli pointed out, the Pope, never capable himself of uniting the peninsula, was always able to keep others from doing so. As spiritual head of a universal church, he had only to request foreign support of his own temporal rule in the papal states.

Italian cosmopolitanism was long coupled with an ardent particularism. Despite (or perhaps because of) their considerable political energies, Italians failed to integrate social interests even within their various states and the brilliant societies of the towns were parasites of the countryside. Traces of this inability to organize urban–rural relations on a basis other than exploitation and oppression have persisted until fairly recently.

Renaissance Italians totally failed to co-ordinate their struggles for independence, and mutual jealousies among the states could not be put aside even in the face of such threats as culminated in the Sack of Rome in 1527. Foreign domination followed; and first Spain and later Austria gained a local preponderance in Italian affairs that was to last until 1870. While the almost tribal strife of the preceding period was to some extent smothered, *divide et impera* was the guiding principle of the European powers. They protected upper-class interests within the states in return for the aristocracy's compliance with their rule and intervened whenever a single Italian state appeared to have ambitions beyond its borders. The period of foreign domination coincided with a time when Mediterranean trade routes were losing importance to those of the Atlantic. The loss of economic stimulus was accompanied by a cultural torpor imposed by foreign rule, and more particularly by the Inquisition, and the vigorous scepticism and speculation characteristic of earlier centuries were silenced. A weakened Italy could hardly conceive of its unification in such circumstances, let alone bring it about.

The Enlightenment and the repercussions of the French Revolution and the Napoleonic conquests altered this situation. Italians, especially in the North, learned the benefits a more rational organization of society could bring. It was during this period that the movement for the political unification of Italy began. This process was successfully completed between 1859 and 1870. But in a sense the Risorgimento achieved only nationhood, not yet unity. Why this should have been so is a matter of some controversy. But it seems clear that two factors are involved: one is the deep-rootedness of imbalance inherited from the past; the other is related to the nature of the Risorgimento. It was, in important respects, an imposition of the North. Juridically, in fact, the Kingdom of Italy thus created was not a new nation at all, but simply an extension of the old Piedmontese Kingdom of the Savoys. More significantly, the Risorgimento was largely a bourgeois movement and the state it created was a bourgeois state. Even though Italy was still almost wholly agricultural, the ruling class was determined to turn the new country into a power able to compete with the rest of Europe. This meant first of all laying the foundations for modern industrialization and creating large armed forces. A large amount of capital was needed to achieve these goals. Since, in contrast to other countries, industrial capital formation on a modern scale had hardly begun, the necessary funds were raised by taxing agriculture. The nature of the goals set was such that their achievement primarily benefited the bourgeoisie of the Northern cities. The result was that the countryside in general, and the Mezzogiorno in particular, failed to reap the fruits of a new economic development for which they were paying more than their share. At the same time governments refused even to consider the existence of a special Mezzogiorno problem, and bought off protest by giving employment to that class of southerners which might normally have forced action.

Thus the initially significant gap between the North and South, between city and country and between social groups, grew further. But the geographical and sectoral imbalances which were the result of these policies were aggravated by other problems, partly of a political and moral nature.

Many injustices in the new state were not the inevitable outcome of industrialization. They were largely the consequence of the make-up and attitudes of the political ruling class and the public administration. Thus pressures from rival interest groups on corrupt politicians distorted the impact of protectionist and other measures favouring new industry.

The Government's existence nearly always depended on such a delicate balance within Parliament that discussion of this and other fundamental issues were discouraged. The new state—used and abused by pressure groups—confirmed most Italians' traditional and well-founded view of government as a source of vexation rather than a protector of collective interests; and their unwillingness to participate—or belief in the impossibility of doing so effectively—gave the power groups which were running the state free play to strengthen their hold.

Fascism subsequently imposed a degree of apparent calm and unity on a divided country, but achieved this only through authoritarianism and oppression. The persistence of deep sectoral, regional, and social divisions became apparent again immediately the fascist regime fell and presented themselves as problems for resolution in the post-war Republic.

PART ONE

ECONOMIC GROWTH AND FLUCTUATIONS

CHAPTER 1

THE MAIN PHASES OF DEVELOPMENT

(i) THE IMMEDIATE POST-WAR PERIOD

As the Second World War ended, the Italian authorities were confronted by a plethora of economic—and political—problems requiring immediate action and/or basic policy decisions. Immediately, they faced acute shortages of many commodities and galloping inflation co-existing with mass unemployment,* and an industrial structure disrupted by war damage and dismantling. Moreover, fighting had continued longer in the South than in the North, thus delaying the resumption of peace-time activity in the poorest part of the country and accentuating the contrasts between its two main regions. These might reasonably be seen as 'emergency' problems, though clearly the problems of unemployment and under-employment, and in particular of extending economic development to the South, could only be alleviated, not solved, in the short term.

In addition, basic decisions were needed on the future structure of the economic system and the desired mechanism and pattern of economic development. A long period of protectionism followed by war had produced an autarkic and strictly government-regulated economic system; agriculture was excessively concentrated on cereals production; the industrial structure was dominated by the traditional, and technologically backward, branches such as food-processing and textiles, while the 'modern' sections—such as steel, chemicals, and the motor-car industry—were small and, with the exception of the last-named, technologically outdated. Industrial growth and modernization were bound

* Unemployment in the whole of Italy was estimated at 2·4 million persons or 12 per cent of the active population. In the South, the unemployment ratios were put as high as 17·5 per cent.

to imply increased dependence on foreign trade, given Italy's meagre endowment in such essential raw materials as timber, coal, iron ore, and petroleum; it could also be argued that increased trade dependence was essential for economically efficient industrialization, since the Italian home market alone could not immediately absorb a sufficient volume of the products of many branches of 'modern' industry to permit economies of scale and specialization to be realized.

It was, however, soon apparent that the post-war picture had some positive features. With the major exception of steel capacity, war damage to industrial plant turned out to be much less far-reaching than had at first appeared; and it was eventually estimated not to exceed 8–10 per cent of capacity. Reconstruction and recovery would benefit from the availability of an ample, cheap, and high-quality labour supply as well as from a high degree of labour mobility which followed from demobilization and the uprooting of large masses of the population. Moreover wartime upheavals, followed by the collapse of a political system and defeat, helped to break down traditional patterns of outlook and behaviour; it was easy to accept a need to 'shape the future' in the absence of the practical possibility of a 'return to normal'.

Two opposing views, partly reflecting political divisions between the right and the left, confronted each other on the best policies for speeding up reconstruction and, more fundamentally, on the choices which would determine the future pattern of development. On the one side were the members of the 'liberal' camp, who identified controls, protectionism, and autarky with the fascist past, with excessive bureaucratic power and ample scope for red tape, corruption, and arbitrary decisions; they believed that only a rapid restoration of a free market mechanism and the opening up of international trade could provide a cure for the ills of the Italian economy. These views were shared by many representatives of the 'modern' industrial sector, who saw export expansion—and readily available imports—as essential to the enlargement of their operations; and the more general economic arguments for a 'liberal' policy—in terms of competitive pressures and allocative efficiency—were also advanced.

The opposing factions advocated a managed and planned economy in the longer run and, immediately, the maintenance of controls: rationing to guarantee an equitable distribution of scarce consumer goods, and foreign exchange controls to allocate export receipts to priority imports.

There was controversy also over the major sources of inflation, and hence over the way in which it was to be brought to a halt. The supporters of a controlled economy favoured mopping up excess liquidity through a currency reform, on the assumption that this would also largely represent a taxation of speculative profits. The 'liberals' believed that government expenditure was the main culprit and that confiscation of private balances or forced loans would amount to a penalty on saving; this would undermine the economic and social status of the middle class, destroy confidence, and dry up a major source for future financing of public expenditure.

The liberal viewpoint carried the day; and progressive dismantling of controls and the rebuilding of market mechanisms was accompanied by speculation on commodity and financial markets and new twists of the price spiral. Only when inflation had assumed intolerable proportions and the balance of payments deteriorated sharply (mainly as a result of a worsening of the food balance) was serious counteraction taken—to reduce liquidity by a partial freezing of bank deposits and to increase imports substantially by using foreign exchange reserves. While the use of orthodox monetary deflation proved highly successful in terms of the immediate objective of price stabilization, it involved heavy cost in terms of potential investment and employment opportunities foregone, and an interruption of the reconstruction process.

On the external front, trade and foreign exchange allocation were progressively liberalized. Exporters were authorized to retain 50 per cent of their export proceeds for disposal on the free market while surrendering the remainder to the authorities at an official rate; and this meant that control over the composition of imports was largely determined by immediate market forces rather than by consideration of the longer-run requirements of the economy. The creation of two foreign exchange markets also led to a regime of multiple exchange rates, differing both between the free and the controlled markets and within the controlled market, with accompanying distortions and speculation. In the free market there was a progressive *de facto* devaluation of the lira which, it was argued by the opponents of the liberal course, did not raise export receipts since demand was inelastic in conditions of universal shortages in Italian export markets. But by 1948 U.S. aid had come to the support of the Italian economy and currency, and the process of liberalization and integration into the western European trading area was thereafter pursued, through the adherence of Italy to the O.E.E.C. and the European Payments Union and, eventually, the full convertibility of the lira.

On the production side, the foundations of modern motor-car, steel, and chemicals industries were laid during the early post-war years. The existence of a large state-controlled industrial sector made it possible for the Government to invest in modernization of steel-making processes and in natural gas production, two basic sectors which played a major role in subsequent industrial development. Within private industry, the modernization and expansion of the motor-car and chemicals branches turned them into leaders of technological progress, well able to stand up to international competition.

The policy choices made during the reconstruction period provided a strong stimulus to the type of export-oriented development which characterized the Italian economy in the subsequent years of rapid industrial transformation and growth. However, they also accentuated or laid the foundations for a number of structural problems which continue to beset the Italian economy to this day.

It could be persuasively argued that the structural problems of the Italian economy could not have been avoided, or alleviated, within a free market economy and without purposeful intervention by public authorities employing, from an early date, at least planning methods, institutions, and instruments akin to those used in France. But the first Italian five-year plan began to operate only in 1966 and was, anyway, ineffectual (see Part Two).

On the other hand, and rather ironically, the decision to dismantle controls and rely on an essentially 'market' system of economic management eventually provided no less scope than before for bureaucratic mismanagement, red tape, and corruption. No more in Italy than in any other modern economy can Government in fact escape the responsibility for administering relatively large sectors of the economy and for influencing, more or less directly, still more sectors. If policy decisions are not organically linked to clear objectives on the one side and to efficient instruments on the other, the scope for inefficiency and abuse is likely to be considerable, and has proved so in Italy.

(ii) RAPID AND SUSTAINED GROWTH, 1951–1963[1]

In the two decades of the 1950s and 1960s taken together, the Italian rate of expansion of gross national product was exceeded in western Europe only by that of the German Federal Republic. Yet, contrary to the view generally held, the Italian 'economic miracle' was really concentrated in the brief period from 1959 to 1963. Before that, if one looks at the years from 1954 onwards—with both post-war reconstruction and post-Korea disturbances by then in the past—one can see that annual growth rates of GDP in Italy were not particularly high in relation to those registered in 'good' years in other western European countries; nor were they high in relation to Italy's output potential. But while most countries experienced sharp fluctuations in growth rates, Italy maintained a remarkably even progress (see Fig. 1), and even the recession which hit most countries in 1958 produced only a mild and short-lived slow-down in Italy. In general the timing of cyclical fluctuations in Italy has been different from that in most other industrial countries. Thus, as periods of recession or slow-down in Italy have coincided with high levels of demand in her main export markets, exports have tended to support economic activity when domestic demand has weakened.

But the 'economic miracle' came to an end in 1963 as recession, lasting into 1965, followed an inflationary boom. A four-year period of renewed but uneasy expansion followed; but a wage explosion at the end of 1969 accompanied by acute social unrest initiated a second recession and a structural crisis, the extent and ramifications of which are not indicated by figures of aggregate output. The average annual rate of growth registered since 1963 is lower than in the earlier period and no longer particularly high by western European standards (see Table 1).

In the years of rapid and sustained growth from 1951 to 1963, exports and fixed-capital formation were the most dynamic elements in total demand (see Fig. 2). Over this period aggregate demand (satisfied by the growth of GNP *plus* imports) rose at an annual rate of 6·3 per cent; exports contributed 1·2 points of this over-all growth and fixed-capital formation 1·5 points, with the relative importance of exports increasing after 1955. In the later years, from 1963 to 1972, as can be seen from the figure, the relative importance of exports increased still more, and, of the 5·3 per cent annual increase of aggregate demand in these years, exports contributed 2·1 points and fixed investment only 0·6 points.

Private consumption rose more slowly than either total demand or GNP up to about 1960, at more or less the same rate as GNP for the next five years, and more rapidly thereafter. Public consumption grew more slowly than GNP virtually throughout the twenty years.

The years up to 1963 were characterized also by a high degree of price stability. Consumer prices increased moderately in most years, and wholesale prices of non-agricultural goods fluctuated year by year, tending even to fall very slightly over the period. Export unit values also fell in most years, thus strengthening the competitive position of Italian goods in export markets.

This price stability doubtless owed something to the apparent decline in unit values of imports in most years. But money wage rates in manufacturing industry also rose rather slowly and, with no significant wage drift, hourly earnings matched this trend; labour productivity rose faster than average earnings and unit labour costs declined.

Italy's increasing integration into the international economy was reflected in a rise in the ratio of imports to GNP from 7·4 per cent in 1951–2 to 14·3 per cent in 1961–2, and increases in the exports/GNP ratio from 6·2 per cent to 14·5 per cent. This increasing trade dependence brought no balance-of-payments difficulties in its train: a small current account surplus was registered by 1957 and a substantial one in 1958, and comfortable surpluses continued for some years thereafter, supplemented by rising long-term capital in-flows ensuring sizeable surpluses on all non-monetary transactions.

The rapid increases of foreign trade had both direct and indirect significance for economic growth in the 1950s and early 1960s. Rising exports were based upon, and themselves stimulated, investment in the export industries. The shift to new export products—such as motor vehicles and chemicals—required investment in new processes to close the technological gap between the Italian and competing foreign industries; larger markets required rationalization in industry and mass production methods.

The rising volume of exports appears to have outweighed the affect on output of the 'leakage' of domestic demand to rapidly expanding imports. Giorgio Fuà estimates that had government revenues and expenditure and private consumption remained at their 1950 levels and foreign trade increased as it actually did from 1950 to 1961, the rise in GNP at current prices would have been 7·4 billion lire instead of the actual 13·3 billion: had other components of demand changed as they actually did but foreign trade remained at its 1950 level, GNP in 1961 would have been

8·7 billion lire more than in 1950.[2] Such calculations can easily be questioned, but one may readily credit the growth of imports itself with some indirectly stimulating impact on the economy, by providing the inputs without which some new lines of production could not have been started or others expanded.

As has been mentioned, rapidly growing exports permitted economic growth without balance-of-payments problems or, therefore, any need for restrictionist policies motivated by such problems as have frequently interrupted the process of expansion in some other countries, notably the United Kingdom. Although private consumption grew at a relatively moderate rate—by comparison with exports—the diversification of consumer demand, and its shift towards cars and household durables as incomes rose, also had a stimulating effect on investment; and the authorities reinforced the autonomous stimuli by offering fiscal incentives for investment and pursuing an expansionist monetary policy.

A more tangible, but nevertheless important, factor in the investment boom was the outburst of entrepreneurship in the new atmosphere of freedom following the constrictions of the pre-war and wartime years. As in West Germany, the break with the past was a shock that provided a new challenge and released latent entrepreneurial energies.

The availability of an ample, and under-utilized, labour supply had several major consequences for the pace and pattern of expansion:

(i) A massive outflow of labour from low-productivity sectors, and particularly from agriculture, to expanding higher-productivity sectors raised over-all labour productivity.

(ii) Large-scale unemployment (the officially recorded unemployment ratio was close to 9 per cent of the labour force in 1951) weakened the bargaining position of the trade unions and wages increased less fast than productivity, at least in the advanced and dynamic branches of industry.

(iii) This resulted in high profits, buoyant business expectations, and a high propensity to invest while substantial enterprise savings and a liberal credit policy provided the necessary finance for a large and rapidly growing volume of investment.

(iv) A shift of income distribution away from wages and in favour of company profits helped to reduce somewhat the share of private consumption in total income and, with a falling share of public consumption, to make room for the larger investment share without inflationary pressures.

(v) Stable or declining wage costs per unit of industrial output allowed high profit levels to be combined with relatively stable prices at home and effective competition in export markets.

In considering the 'supply side' of economic growth in this period, one cannot do better than quote E. F. Denison's path-breaking study of the sources of growth in eight European countries and the U.S.A.[3]

Percentage contribution to expansion of gross domestic product in each period

	1950–62	1950–5	1955–62
Total factor input	*28*	*31*	*26*
Labour	16	22	12
Capital	12	9	14
Output per unit of input	*72*	*69*	*74*
Advances in knowledge[1]	13	12	13
Changes in the lag of application of knowledge, etc.	15	22	9
Improved allocation of resources	24	19	28
of which: contraction of agricultural inputs	17	14	20
Economies of scale	21	16	24
Total	100	100	100

1. Advances in technological and managerial knowledge, including business organization.

From: E. F. Denison, *Why Growth Rates Differ* (Brookings Institution, Washington, D.C., 1967; © 1967 by the Brookings Institution, Washington, D.C.).

International comparisons of such data must be viewed with caution; but it seems that the contribution to growth of returns to factor inputs has been highest in Italy among all the countries studied, with the sole exception of France. To be noted are the substantial contributions to growth of changes in the lag of the application of knowledge (catching up with technologies applied elsewhere) during 1950–5, of improved allocation of resources—largely due to a massive outflow of labour from agriculture—and of economies of scale, the last two of increasing importance during 1955–62.

(iii) A DIGRESSION ON STRUCTURAL PROBLEMS

When the first major setback to rapid economic expansion hit the Italian economy in 1963–5, a number of leading Italian economists had already expressed concern about serious structural imbalances in the Italian economic and social system.[4] They pointed to widespread manifestations of structural disequilibria inherited from the past, which had not been reduced but rather accentuated during the period of the 'economic miracle', and to the development of new strains as a by-product, or in some instances the logical consequence, of the *pattern* of growth and the policies pursued in shaping that pattern.

The post-war economic expansion, which had been based on the development of modern and competitive industries and which had successfully averted the danger of any balance-of-payments constraint on rapid growth of domestic demand and output, was also largely responsible for the appearance and/or accentuation of an economic and social dualism. This was manifest in a tendency for a widening of gaps between regions—most of all between the South and the North-West of Italy—between agriculture and industry, and between industrial branches—especially between the 'exposed' export-oriented and the 'sheltered' home-market industries.

Among other adverse developments, it was argued, were distortions in the pattern of consumption—imbalances both between private and collective consumption and between the various categories of private consumption; inappropriate allocation of investment resources—regionally, sectorally, and between private and social infra-structure investment; and, finally, an inequitable income distribution.

But the two major and lasting preoccupations were the chronic under-employment of labour, as industry and tertiary activities failed to absorb all of the massive outflow of workers from agriculture and, partly connected with this, the failure to reduce the development gap between South and North. Moreover, large-scale internal migrations of labour, attracted by better employment opportunities in the North and in industrial centres in general had brought in their wake rapid and chaotic urban development, with the associated high economic and social costs and tensions.

While the existence of an industrial dualism and of other structural imbalances in the Italian economic system was widely recognized, there were—and are—divergent opinions as to the causal connections between the growth process and these phenomena. One view holds that they were all linked to the Italian export-led pattern of development.[5] It is argued that the Italian industrial structure had been largely based in the past on traditional industries—food, textiles, wood processing, etc.—for which international demand was now expanding only slowly. Thus rapid export expansion required industrial adaptation to match the demand pattern of the most highly developed industrial countries—a shift in the Italian industrial structure towards technologically advanced, high-productivity, and capital-intensive industries such as the metal-using branches, and chemicals. But this also meant the development of a pattern of output which was out of line with the composition of consumer demand in a still relatively low-income country. Export-propelled growth thus resulted in the splitting of the economy into two major, divergent segments: a competitive, highly efficient, technologically progressive industrial sector, which provided only limited expansion of employment opportunities, and a sheltered home-market sector with predominantly backward and inefficient methods of production and only slowly rising productivity but with a large absorptive capacity for labour.

From this fundamental split most of the other structural distortions were derived: the regional concentration of modern industry in the North accentuating the development gap between North and South; the self-reinforcing mechanism of high-productivity increases in the advanced export sector, slow growth of labour costs, high profits, ample self-financing possibilities, high investment, and further expansion contrasting with the reverse process in the backward sectors; inequalities in pay and personal incomes and divergent price developments in the 'modern' and 'traditional' sectors; the anomaly of a private consumption pattern where rapid increases in expenditure on high-quality and luxury goods co-existed with inadequate satisfaction of essential needs; and the failure of public expenditure to provide collective services such as low-cost housing, health services, education, urban transport, etc., in satisfactory quality and quantity.

The attribution of many of the dual-economy characteristics and other distortions of the Italian economic structure to a common cause—a largely export-geared expansion—is quite convincing. But it might be asked what other pattern of development could have been envisaged which would have reconciled on the one hand an over-all growth rate sufficient to absorb vast idle manpower resources and to raise average *per capita* income to a level beginning to approach that of other industrial countries in western Europe, with, on the other, a more balanced expansion, better suited to an economy which was still situated half-way between the advanced industrial and the developing countries.

The short answer is, probably, that in an essentially free, though imperfect, market system such a reconciliation could hardly be achieved. Experience elsewhere suggests that neither within a single economy nor internationally can rapid development of richer regions be relied upon by itself to pull up the levels of the poorer, and certainly not to improve their *relative* position: within industrial sectors and within regions prosperity and decline have strong self-perpetuating characteristics. The distribution of income among social groups, determined by market forces and relative bargaining strengths, may change as a consequence of rapid structural change in the economy; but again there is little *a priori* reason to assume that the end-result will be greater social or regional equality.

To avoid the economic and social strains existing today in the Italian economy would have required far more carefully planned and far-reaching action by the authorities than was ever in serious prospect. Such action should have been based on a forward-looking vision of the desirable geographic and sectoral pattern of output and employment and of the foreseeable individual and social needs of a modern economy. A major cause of the troubles to come was the failure of governments to take a long-term view of objectives and priorities. They might have planned to use the opportunity offered by prospective rapid additions to aggregate wealth and income to re-allocate at least part of the increments so as to improve the distribution pattern. They might have tried to mobilize the competing social groups into a co-operative effort.

Today structural imbalances and social and political tensions impose upon society and its governments more urgent problems than can possibly all be resolved simultaneously and quickly. This explosive situation might have been avoided had sufficient efforts been made in time.

The underlying strains were manifest by the time the smooth development process of the 1950s was interrupted by the 1963 inflation and subsequent recession; they were not relieved during the subsequent phase of hesitant upturn between 1966 and 1969, and they helped to produce disruptive social and political strife during the protracted crisis which followed the 'hot autumn' of 1969.

The mounting difficulties of the last few years are now generally recognized as manifestations of profound structural and institutional maladjustments, rather than mere conjunctural setbacks which can be corrected with the help of traditional demand-management policies. But the two aspects of the unsatisfactory performance of the Italian economy since 1963 and of the recent protracted recession are closely interrelated, structural problems reinforcing the cyclical downturns, and the latter rendering the elimination of structural weaknesses even more difficult.

A more detailed analysis of some of the structural problems confronting Italian policy- and decision-makers and the way in which they have been handled, and generally have failed to be solved, is presented in Part Two. For the present, we may note that intensifying structural problems underlay short-term economic developments from 1963 onwards.

(iv) INFLATION AND RECESSION: 1963–1965

After a decade of rapid and remarkably stable growth (interrupted only briefly in 1958), price stability, and balance-of-payments equilibrium, the Italian economy experienced an inflationary boom in 1963, followed by a sharp slow-down in the rate of expansion in 1964. GNP growth had already slowed down between 1962 and 1963, and it reached its lowest rate of 2·9 per cent in 1964, accelerating only slightly in 1965. The recession was short-lived but acute, and the effectiveness of hitherto untried instruments for short-term demand management was put to the test for the first time. The novelty of this setback produced a shock to confidence which might appear excessive, compared with the reactions to similar developments in other industrial countries, where repeated ups and downs of the business cycle had by then become familiar.* Political uncertainties, resulting from the taking over of the Government by the 'Centro-Sinistra' coalition after protracted and laborious negotiations, and the nationalization of electric power production in 1962 added to the feeling of unease among the entrepreneurial class and other economic and social groups.

The Italian economy had been under strain since the

* One of the leading Italian economists, Francesco Forte, devoted some 500 pages to a description and analysis of this phase in *La Congiuntura in Italia, 1961–1965*, Etas Kompass, Milan, 1966.

beginning of 1962. Full employment and scarcities of some types of skilled labour had begun to make themselves felt in the industrial centres of the North, even though unemployment and under-employment remained substantial in other regions and some low-paid and low-productivity activities—e.g. agriculture, retail distribution, and the public administration—were obviously over-manned. This produced a radical change in the economic and social climate of the country. Pressure on the labour market strengthened the trade unions' bargaining power and encouraged demands for larger wage increases, motivated also by consciousness of higher or more rapidly rising wage levels in other industrial countries. The trade-union federations began to co-operate with each other in wage bargaining and also adopted a strategy of decentralized and plant bargaining. The outbreak of the first national strikes was further evidence of new trade-union strength.

The resulting sharp wage increases began to outstrip productivity advances in 1962 and the gap widened in 1963 when growth of productivity slackened. Earnings rose more rapidly than wage rates and unit labour costs in manufacturing which had declined, on average, during the 1950s, began to climb rapidly in 1962 (see Table 4). With wage increases spreading to low-productivity sectors, such as construction and services, unit labour costs increased even more rapidly in those sectors. Furthermore the system of a quarterly adjustment of wages to the cost of living contributed to wage inflation as price increases accelerated.

The rise in labour income and in unit labour costs had several repercussions: on profits and the propensity to invest; on income distribution and the propensity to consume; on prices; on the balance of payments through an upsurge of imports, as rising consumer demand spilled over to foreign supplies, and a marked but brief slow-down of export expansion as domestic demand pressure diverted potential exports to the home market.

Gross fixed-capital formation, which had been rising by some 12 per cent in both 1960 and 1961, slowed down in the two following years and registered substantial declines in 1964 and 1965 (see Table 2). Three partly conflicting influences affected demand for fixed investment: the rapid rise in private consumption and a liberal monetary policy, on the one hand, and the narrowing of profit margins as the rise of unit labour costs accelerated, on the other.[6] With the subsequent tightening of monetary policy, the negative influences on investment demand came to predominate.

The rate of increase in unit labour costs in manufacturing accelerated from 1·2 per cent in 1961 to 5·3 per cent in 1962 and to close to 15 per cent in 1963, and the share of profits in value added in manufacturing declined from 42 per cent to 35 per cent in the same period. Enterprise savings declined and self-financing possibilities were reduced, while access to external finance was rendered more difficult by a restrictive monetary policy. All this had a severe impact on productive investment. Fixed-capital expenditure on machinery and plant fell by as much as 19 per cent both in 1964 and in 1965, and the corresponding falls in investment in transport equipment were 12 per cent and 5 per cent. Reinforcing the impact of falling profit margins, political factors and the nationalization of an important sector (electricity supply) produced a climate of mistrust and defeatism.

Moreover, public sector investment behaved in a pro-cyclical manner during this period. General government investment (admittedly, a very small part of the total) declined and the capital expenditure of public corporations also reinforced rather than offset the behaviour of the private sector (see Fig. 3).*

International competition prevented producers in exposed sectors from passing on the whole of cost increases to prices, so that export prices rose very moderately; but the hitherto slow increase of consumer prices accelerated to 7 per cent in 1963, and wholesale prices for non-agricultural goods, which had declined in several earlier years, registered their first sharp increase (5 per cent).

* For a discussion of the special structure and functions of public corporations see Part Two.

The wage explosion produced an enormous rise in aggregate incomes of employed labour (38 per cent in the two years 1962 and 1963 taken together) and a shift in their share in total national income from 51 per cent in 1961 to 58 per cent in 1964, while the corresponding share of independent traders fell from 34 per cent to 31 per cent. The retained profits of corporations (after payment of dividends, etc., and taxes) fell from 2·9 per cent to 0·9 per cent of the national income (see Table 5).

The government sector contributed to the massive increase in dependent labour income, by granting large wage concessions early in the period; and this had a particularly strong impact on income distribution as about one-third of all dependent (wage and salary) employment was under the direct or indirect control of the public authorities. At the same time, public wage and salary increases, conceded on a large scale and within a short span of time, had a strong and widely diffused cost-raising effect in that they were not matched by corresponding increases in efficiency or (long overdue) rationalization and modernization of public activities.

Shifts in income distribution, so substantial and so concentrated in time, had a large impact on the propensity to consume and the savings ratio; and this, on top of still-expanding investment and export demand in 1963, produced strong pressures on resources and the first manifestations of a demand inflation in the post-war period.

Consumer expenditure at constant prices rose by 9 per cent in 1963, compared with an average annual rate of increase of 5 per cent from 1952 to 1962, and a large part of the additional consumer demand fell on sectors of relatively inelastic supply—such as higher-quality foods—thus reinforcing the pressure on consumer prices. The rapid growth of incomes tended to change the composition of private consumption, as large numbers of wage-earners entered higher-income groups and began to adopt the more advanced patterns of consumption typical of highly developed industrial countries; and mass migrations to towns further accentuated the shift towards higher-quality foods, household durables, and motor vehicles.

The balance of payments had begun to weaken by the end of 1962 as demand pressures spilled over on to imports (see Table 6). A considerable portion of the increase of imports consisted of foodstuffs, as a short-fall of maize and olive crops and adverse conditions for livestock production raised imports in the short run. But the shift of consumption to new food categories would have raised import requirements even had food production not suffered a temporary setback.

With exports slowing down as a result of the greater pull of the home market, the trade deficit more than doubled in a year—to reach $1,903 million in 1963. In addition, there was a substantial rise in the outflow of long-term capital, from $298 million to $542 million, caused by the confidence factors already mentioned and also by a stock exchange crisis and anticipation of a new tax on dividends. The overall balance of payments turned from a balance in 1962 into an unprecedented deficit of $1,250 million.

The novelty of the inflation experience gave rise to a great deal of discussion and controversy as to its causes. One widely held opinion was that it was due to the wage explosion, which had eroded profits and compelled entrepreneurs to pass on cost increases to prices and, at the same time, had produced a consumer buying spree.

The opposite view, held by representatives of trade unions and of the left, was that the rapid rise in wages represented a long-overdue catching-up process after a protracted period of wage restraint; the blame for the inflation must be put on entrepreneurs and the inappropriate use they made of their past large profits. They had proceeded on the contradictory assumptions that they would be able to rely on an ample labour supply and that wages, seen as costs, would continue to rise only moderately whereas incomes, seen as effective demand, would grow rapidly. With a lack of foresight, they had failed to adopt an appropriate investment policy which would have raised productivity sufficiently rapidly to absorb cost increases. What neither view appeared to realize was that in inflationary conditions, incorporating sharp increases in real wages, a clash between enterprise interests and the interests of the economy as a whole was liable to arise as production processes became too labour-intensive from a cost point of view and attempts to reduce labour-intensity risked aggravating the employment problem.

Other observers considered that to launch accusations at either trade-union organizations or the entrepreneurial class alone neither was justified nor pointed to the heart of the matter. Both groups had simply availed themselves as best they could of existing market opportunities, in the absence of any constraining framework of long-term objectives and policy measures. A link was seen between the short-term difficulties of the Italian economy and its underlying structural distortions. Thus it cannot be argued, in the light of Italy's earlier high domestic savings ratio, that a shortage of capital had prevented more productivity-raising investment. But, first, a fairly large proportion of domestic savings had been exported in the years between 1958 and 1963, and this tendency was to become more accentuated from 1964 onwards (see Fig. 4); secondly, major blame for the difficulties suddenly emerging could be placed on the use which had been made of savings at home. A notable part was channelled to non-productive investment—such as speculation in land and building—or to investments which produced neither lasting employment nor productivity increases. In agriculture, for example, wasteful investment projects were undertaken in areas with little prospect for future development; some infra-structure investment had been undertaken with little regard to the foreseeable location of complementary activities.

As to the explosion of wage demands and private consumption, a mitigating influence might have been exerted by measures to stimulate household savings and by the provision of attractive investment outlets for such savings, but far more helpful would have been earlier, and much more substantial, well-selected and well-located public expenditures on the provision of collective services and social infra-structures so as to raise standards of living by means other than a disorderly increase of individual incomes and consumption.[7]

The year 1964 brought radical changes in the economic situation, as a combined outcome of spontaneous tendencies and of restrictive economic policy measures. The growth rate of GNP dwindled to a mere 2·9 per cent (a negligible figure by past Italian standards) and gross fixed-capital formation fell by 6·4 per cent. The advance of aggregate output—such as it was—was largely due to agriculture, while industrial production declined sharply in the course of the year, particularly in the investment goods industries.

The decline of productive investment reduced employment and the rate of growth of the wage bill, and raised unemployment; shorter working hours and smaller wage drift had a further adverse impact on labour income, and this, in turn, checked the previous rapid expansion of consumer demand.

On the other hand, as hourly earnings in manufacturing continued to rise (by 11 per cent) at a rate considerably outpacing productivity increases, unit wage costs still exerted strong pressures on profit margins, and prices continued to advance rapidly (see Tables 3 and 4).

On the whole, the situation in 1964 did not differ much from that of 1963 from the point of view of price and wage developments and the profitability of enterprises. But in terms of aggregate output, investment and consumer demand and employment, the 1963 boom had given way to a downturn, even though an acceleration of exports (from a 6·9 per cent rise in 1963 to an 11·6 per cent increase in 1964), attributable partly to booming demand in the economies of Italy's main trading partners, put a floor under the recession. The slack domestic demand was reflected in a steep decline of imports, and the trade deficit was reduced by about one-third; there was a reversal in net long-term capital movements and the over-all balance on non-monetary transactions turned into a surplus of nearly $800 million.

In a brief span of time, the Italian economy had moved abruptly from a phase of demand and cost inflation to a situation in which cost inflation persisted in conditions of slackening demand. The lower turning-point of the recession was reached in the first quarter of 1965, recovery starting in some sectors of production while over-all employment and investment continued to decline. It was only in the last months of 1965 that renewed expansion gathered momentum and productive investment began to turn upwards. Exports accelerated further in 1965 and, with progressive increases in current public expenditures (mainly transfers) and public investment, provided strong supports to rising total activity.

As demand weakened, price increases eventually became more moderate; and the rise in wages also slowed down in the course of the year, as the moderation of cost-of-living increases reduced the frequency and size of automatic wage adjustments and also because no major collective agreements became due for renewal.

The improvement in the balance of payments registered in 1964 continued into 1965; visible trade flows were just in surplus—an exceptional event in the history of Italian external transactions. The current account surplus rose from \$620 million in 1964 to \$2,209 million and with a capital outflow of \$455 (largely due to export credits and payments lag following on the shift of the trade balance) the balance on non-monetary transactions ran a surplus of \$1,594 million. This was the highest so far reached, and the international reserve position strengthened substantially (see Table 6). All in all, conditions appeared favourable for a vigorous upturn at the end of 1965.

Adjustment of the labour market to the recession

A feature which is peculiar to the dual character, both sectorally and regionally, of the Italian economy is the behaviour of the labour market in the different phases of the business cycle; and some aspects of this behaviour seem to have become a permanent and structural characteristic (see Table 7 and Part Two).

In conditions of high activity and strong demand, the

Italian labour market reacted in the following way: there was an increase of employment in manufacturing and construction; an accelerated outflow from rural occupations to urban employment; a moderate reduction of employment in services and handicrafts and a shift from self-employment to dependent employment, and a considerable reduction in the total labour force. The last, surprising phenomenon is due to the fact that, with a massive exodus from agriculture, persons statistically recorded as employed—largely under-employed women and young persons—left the labour force and became part of the non-active population. The change in the employment structure involved a shift from low- to high-productivity sectors and contributed towards raising over-all productivity and maintaining high growth rates.

In recession, a number of adjustments took place which made the employment situation appear much less disturbing than it was in reality and than might have been expected in the light of the slackening of demand and output growth. What happened—and this was not evident from over-all employment and unemployment data—was a marked worsening in the *pattern* of employment. Open unemployment increased less than might have been expected because the outflow from agriculture slowed down considerably, industry reacted by shortening hours worked rather than by dismissing workers, and there was a substantial absorption of labour by some service sectors, as people who failed to find employment in industry drifted to often precarious jobs in marginal activities.

Some of these shifts in the pattern of employment in 1964 became more accentuated in 1965 even though a slight upturn had already begun. Thus in the labour market the 1964–5 recession was reflected mainly in a check to the previous move to high-productivity sectors, or in a return to low-productivity and low-income sectors, and hence in a considerable misallocation and/or under-utilization of labour resources.

The recession had a particularly severe impact on the employment pattern of the South as the main emigration area of agricultural labour to other sectors and regions. Net migration to the North slowed down and there was also some re-immigration, while employment in 'various services' increased sharply after a steady decline for five consecutive years. Since the marginal service activities had already suffered from overcrowding in the past, this, together with the check to the outflow from agriculture, had a retarding effect on the progress towards higher productivity and incomes so urgently needed in the region.

Economic policies

The predominating tendency of monetary policy in Italy has been expansionary, though with two major interruptions to this general course—the first in 1963–4 and the second in 1969–70.

At the beginning of 1962, when inflationary strains had already begun to make themselves felt, the monetary authorities nevertheless supported the existing level of demand by increasing liquidity, in the belief that un-utilized or under-utilized resources in some sectors of the economy would prevent price increases and that international reserves provided a safe enough margin for further expansion. Moreover, when the balance of payments turned into deficit, commercial banks were authorized to borrow abroad and this offset the contractionary effect of the deficit. Thus monetary policy tended to contribute to the demand inflation.

Policy was reversed only in September 1963, when investment demand had already begun to weaken spontaneously; but the blame for the delay cannot be put on the monetary authorities. The Governor of the Bank of Italy had advocated the adoption of restrictive measures much earlier. When action to reduce the growth of bank credit was eventually initiated, the commercial banks were soon instructed also to discontinue their borrowing abroad.

In 1964, although the economy had moved into a recession and the balance of payments into surplus, the authorities at first reinforced their deflationary policies. Over-all monetary restraint was tightened and fiscal measures came to the support of monetary instruments only at this late stage. Indirect taxes on motor-cars and petrol were raised and subsequently all turnover tax rates were increased. In addition, shock imports of butter and meat, to be sold at government-controlled prices, were intended to keep down consumer prices of some essential goods.

To strengthen the external position, credit facilities of $1 billion were obtained in March 1964 from the U.S. Treasury, some banking institutions, and several western European central banks; and in addition a $225 million credit was granted by the I.M.F. The total roughly corresponded to the loss of international reserves in 1963.

With demand pressures evidently weakening, but price and wage increases continuing, a cautious change-over from a deflationary to a reflationary course was started in the summer of 1964 and gradually reinforced until late in 1965. Credit restraint was progressively eased, with particular emphasis on investment financing. To assist small and medium-sized enterprises which are usually most affected by a credit squeeze, a special fund of 100 billion lire was set up; the Ministerial Credit Committee gave authorizations for important capital issues; the Central Bank provided indirect finance for investment by public corporations so as to reduce their calls on the capital market.

As to budgetary policy, efforts were made to raise public expenditure in 1965, through an acceleration both of public works and of public enterprise investment. But, in fact, both these categories of investment declined in 1965. Most of the expansionary impact of general government action was due to the temporary shift of employers' liability for social security payments to the budget, an increase in public salaries (decided upon earlier), and the raising of pensions.*

* The so-called 'fiscalization' of social security contributions for a period is an important weapon in the arsenal of Italian policy instruments. Its usefulness for short-term demand management is obvious but might be weakened or disappear if proposals put forward at various times for a permanent transfer of such liabilities to the budget are implemented. But there are other arguments in favour of such a change (see below).

These last two measures had no deliberately reflationary purpose.

Even though the total contribution of general government financing and expenditure to GNP growth was higher in 1965 than ever before (or after), its inadequacy can be shown by the fact that a substantial gap between actual and potential output had developed in 1964 and been maintained in 1965 and 1966 (see Fig. 5).

The effect of most of these measures (both monetary and budgetary) was slow to materialize and began to be felt only in the second half of 1965. While monetary restraint had been successful enough—and probably too successful in view of the earlier spontaneous slackening of investment demand—in checking capital expenditure, private investment failed to respond to subsequent monetary stimulation in conditions of flagging demand, low profits, and poor business expectations, even though exports grew faster in 1965 than in 1964.

Experience of demand-management policies in this period was not dissimilar to that of many other countries at about the same time or earlier. Action was hesitant and belated; measures were applied piecemeal and *ad hoc*, in response to uncertain diagnosis of economic indicators which often reflected past rather than current tendencies, or in response to unavoidable pressures. Common to other countries also was the asymmetry of the impact of monetary instruments, invoking strong response in periods of restraint, and a weak and slow response—as long as aggregate demand failed to recover for other reasons—in periods of stimulation. These generally familiar features are the more understandable given that the Italian authorities had so far had little experience of evaluating the interactions of economic variables for the purpose of attempts to change economic trends, and that they were handling relatively untried weapons for dealing with inflation and recession, complicated by the fact that cost and price increases continued into the recessionary phase.

Above all, there was delay in using budgetary instruments

and these were intrinsically weak, both on the taxation and the expenditure side (see Chapter 4). The budget had a mildly expansionary effect on GNP in 1963 and the stimulating impact was reduced in 1964 at a time when monetary policy had shifted towards promoting renewed expansion. But changes in budget revenues and expenditures seem to have been due more to chance factors already mentioned and to the automatic effects of changes in economic activity on the budget than to purposive manipulation. Furthermore, public corporations' investment (which does not figure in budget data) declined in 1964 and 1965 at a time when private business investment had also fallen, thus accentuating rather than mitigating the recession (see Figs. 3 and 5).

It was at this juncture, with experience of cost inflation continuing in the face of stagnating demand and employment, that an incomes policy was advocated for the first time. Not surprisingly, such proposals found no favour with the trade unions. It was argued that, with the difficulty in controlling non-wage incomes, with the large share of income from self-employment, and lack of statistical information on profits, the whole burden of such a policy would fall on wage incomes. Resistance to serious consideration of an incomes policy was heightened by awareness of large-scale tax evasion and clandestine capital exports and by the absence of any long-term policy for income redistribution linked with other objectives for planned development and structural change.

Thus the Italian economy emerged from its first significant experience of inflation-turning-to-recession, with the inadequacy of its policy instruments for demand management recognized (the monetary authorities themselves deploring the almost exclusive reliance on monetary measures) but not corrected. The tightening of credit at a time of cost inflation, and the failure of fiscal policy to provide adequate reinforcement for monetary relaxation when demand required to be stimulated, resulted in a loss of industrial investment and employment opportunities, which was particularly damaging in Italian conditions of unemployment and underemployment of labour resources but sharp rises in industrial labour costs. Furthermore, the failure of public sector investment to compensate for the short-fall of private capital expenditure not only accentuated the conjunctural fluctuations but also rendered the long-term structural deficiencies of the Italian economy more acute.

CHAPTER 2

THE RECENT DEVELOPMENT CRISIS

(i) LONGER-TERM TENDENCIES

The 1964–5 recession was followed by four years of renewed and relatively rapid expansion which might, at the time, have appeared as the resumption of a more 'normal' pace of development. In the event, this upswing turned out to be ephemeral and based on shaky foundations. Looking at the period from 1964 onwards *as a whole*, it is by now evident that the recession initiated an altogether new phase in Italy's post-war economic history—one of chronic and intractable difficulties. In terms of measurable magnitudes, its most marked feature was a sharp check to investment. It took four years for fixed investment to return to its 1963 level; the total investment ratio declined; the share of public investment also diminished, and the social infra-structure became increasingly inadequate. In the period 1966–70 the Italian investment ratio was second-lowest (above that of the United Kingdom) among the nine E.E.C. countries and also for investment in machinery and plant alone (above Luxembourg). At the same time, some 10 to 15 per cent of domestic saving was absorbed by the external surplus from 1964 onwards—that is, it was invested in other countries or in currency reserves (see Fig. 4).

As the figures below suggest, investment accounted for the greater part of the slow-down in the rate of over-all expansion; and the stronger stimulus imparted by exports was offset by the slackening of the remaining sectors of demand, the 'leak' of demand to imports remaining virtually unchanged.

Official statistics show an almost uninterrupted decline in total employment and the total labour force year by year.

This reflects, in part, a disappearance of members of farm households from the recorded 'active population' as the families leave agriculture. But it also reflects a genuine chronic under-utilization of labour resources which is almost certainly understated by recorded unemployment and officially estimated under-employment. Employment

Annual percentage change of gross domestic product and of sectors of demand weighted by their shares in the total (at constant prices)

	1951–8	1959–64	1964–71
Private consumption	2·8	3·8	3·5
Public consumption	0·5	0·6	0·4
Gross investment	1·5	1·5	0·6
Exports	1·0	1·6	2·1
Imports	−0·7	−1·9	−1·8
Gross domestic product	5·1	5·7	4·8

Source: Segretario Generale della Programmazione Economica, Appendix to the 'Rapporto sull'Esperienza di Programmazione' (1973).

in industry, private-sector tertiary activities and public administration did not increase sufficiently to absorb all the manpower released from agriculture and wishing to work.

On the production side, industrial expansion from the 1963 peak to 1972 was slower than before, and the uneven progress of the engineering sectors was particularly noticeable (see Fig. 7). Productivity increases slackened as the contribution of movements of labour from low- to high-productivity sectors became less important, but the rate of productivity growth also slowed within many branches of industry, with a particularly sharp deceleration in chemicals.

A calculation by the O.E.C.D. secretariat suggests that, even in periods of rapid expansion, actual output has been almost continuously below the 'potential' output attainable with relatively full utilization of the existing capital stock and, obviously, still further below what would have been possible with higher rates of investment than were actually achieved.[1] Moreover the gap between actual and potential output widened noticeably after 1964 and remained wide until 1972 (some 6 per cent of actual GDP in that year) with the exception of a brief improvement in 1968–70. Shaky as such calculations must be, they tend to support other evidence that the Government's demand-management policies increasingly failed to realize the economy's potential for growth after 1963, partly because the problems multiplied while the policy instruments were little changed.

(ii) THE TRADE UNIONS AND THE ECONOMIC AND SOCIAL CRISIS

Although economic expansion was resumed in 1965, manifestations of a deeply-rooted social and psychological crisis became increasingly widespread and acute. There were the growing frustrations of large sections of the working population over deteriorating conditions of life for which higher incomes could not compensate; there was the impatience with, and loss of confidence in, the authorities over promises not kept, as political instability, lack of continuity, and institutional and administrative weaknesses rendered policy-making hesitant and postponed urgent reforms. As time went on, social strife and outbursts of violence became endemic.

The growing strains burst out into the open in the autumn of 1969 with a wave of strikes starting with the negotiations for renewal of wage agreements for the three years 1970–2. Although economic growth, and in particular export growth, had accelerated in the earlier part of 1969, trade-union pressures and the subsequent wage explosion cannot be attributed to excess demand or tight labour market conditions. In fact, the unemployment ratio remained roughly unchanged at 3·4 per cent (with total recorded employment falling), there was a substantial export surplus, and price increases remained rather moderate. There is little doubt that the economy was still operating with some slack.

Wage increases had already speeded up before the strikes,

because of the abolition of formal regional differences in rates, sliding-scale adjustments to the cost of living and some new wage settlements; and wage drift had accelerated. The new wage agreements covering some 5 million workers became effective in January 1970 and big jumps in the rates of increase of wage rates, hourly earnings, and unit labour costs followed (Tables 4 and 8). In addition to increases in pay, the agreements provided for a gradual reduction in the standard working week from 43–4 to 40 hours, for increases in fringe benefits, and the extension of trade-union rights to operate inside workshops.

Working hours lost through strikes amounted to 302 million in 1969 (74 million in 1968), 146 million in 1970, 103 million in 1971, and 135 million in 1972. The 'hot autumn' of 1969 initiated a new phase of trade-union activity—one of unremitting pressure. Strikes no longer occurred only in connection with national wage bargaining (and were no longer limited to the period of the wage round) but also at the plant level. Belligerency was no longer linked to conditions of demand pressure and labour shortages; and it has persisted during the latest recession, notwithstanding the existence of ample labour reserves.

The new objectives of the trade-union struggle go far beyond the traditional demands for wage increases, for the reduction of the standard working week, overtime, and shift work, and for the concession of fringe benefits. They have recently also been directed at a wide range of broader aims, involving confrontation not only with employers but also with the public authorities.

There is, in the first place, a growing resistance to the deterioration of conditions both inside and outside the factory. Inside the factory it is directed at the tough pace on the production line, which reflects managements' efforts to raise productivity to compensate for the rapid rise in labour costs. The methods used have often had ill effects on health and safety and have produced psychological stress. Outside the factory, the trade-union fight is aimed at the difficult living conditions created by urban congestion and failure to provide basic facilities. Trade unions protest against inadequate public transport, poor and expensive housing, deficient social services, and the high cost of distribution; they ask for more facilities for professional training and the schooling of workers' children and for an efficient health service.

Beyond these claims directly related to the quality of life of the working population, there is an increasing involvement with more general policy issues. Trade-union representatives ask for workers' participation in economic and social policy decisions. They wish to take an active part in economic planning and in choices affecting the geographic and sectoral distribution of publicly controlled capital expenditure—the choice between social and productive investment, the formulation and carrying out of policies for the development of the South, for the creation of new jobs, and for the speeding up of structural reforms in general. They protest against the excessive inequality of the distribution of income and wealth between social classes, economic categories and regions, and the shocking contrast between pockets of opulence and misery. Other causes of tension are the large pay differentials between different categories of workers and employees, which are neither justified by differences in qualifications or demand–supply conditions nor mitigated by progressive taxation. All these claims reflect a profound social crisis and a general collapse of confidence in the functioning of existing institutions.

It is against this background of accumulated grievances and disillusionment that the last triennial wage-round (end of 1972 to beginning of 1973) must be seen. It took place after a protracted phase of recession, under-utilized capacities, profit squeeze, and rising unemployment; and the climate of uncertainty as to the outcome of the wage negotiations and a renewed strike wave were among the factors causing stagnation of private investment.

The metal-workers' agreement (for both the public and the private sectors) was concluded after many months of difficult negotiations, and strikes involving enormous loss of man-hours worked. It presents many new and revolutionary features, providing for across-the-board wage increases, further limitations of overtime, agreements on job classification, piece-work, and allowances, and an integration of blue- and white-collar workers' wage and salary scales. It stipulates a 39-hour week for steel-workers, which has not been applied so far in any other European country. Workers are to be entitled to 150 hours paid study time each year and another 120 hours unpaid leave for study purposes. It is generally considered virtually impossible to assess the overall cost of these concessions.

In considering the effects of recent developments on future labour costs and enterprise profits, some negative and some positive factors have to be taken into account. On the negative side there was the impact of continuing labour unrest on output and costs in private industry, and the unprecedentedly rapid price increases which produced in 1973 the largest number of cost-of-living wage adjustments ever experienced. On the positive side, more rapid productivity increases have accompanied a recent modest upturn and there are reports of much better working in some major industries (Fiat is one example). There was also some evidence of a more responsible—or cautious—attitude of some trade-union leaders,* though opposition to any concept of a 'social pact' or 'auto-regulation' of strikes has come from a faction of C.I.S.L., the second of the three large trade-union confederations. Instead, participation in the planning process, in employment policies, and in investment decisions for the South have been put forward as a precondition for a more moderate attitude to wage increases and other concessions. If these conditions can be fulfilled

* Thus, for instance, the Secretary-General of C.G.I.L. (the General Confederation of Italian Workers, of left-wing affiliation) stated in an interview in May 1973 that there are certain strikes which should be avoided, not because they are illegitimate but because they do not serve the trade-union movement. If used indiscriminately, strikes can become a boomerang because they isolate the workers and create resentment in public opinion and among other sections of the working population. He distinguished, in particular, between strikes in the industrial sector and those in public services such as tramways and the post-offices which affect the everyday life of the population.

'a big step will have been made towards a modern conception of economic policy and of the important role trade unions can play.'[2]

Further positive factors, affecting the profitability of enterprises in the face of sharp wage-cost increases, were the high rate of inflation in other countries and the *de facto* lira devaluation which have made it easier to pass on cost increases to prices without unduly weakening the competitive power of Italian exports.

(iii) THE RECESSION AND THE INCIPIENT UPTURN: 1969 TO MID-1973

The immediate impact of the 'hot autumn' on domestic demand and output cannot be gathered from the annual data presented in Table 2, but only from half-yearly figures. GNP, which had risen by nearly 9 per cent from the second half of 1968 to the first half of 1969, declined in the second half of that year. Gross fixed investment, particularly in machinery and equipment, was most severely hit; but exports, which had been rising exceptionally fast, also fell. On the whole, domestic demand slackened less than output. In 1970, the slight slow-down of the rate of expansion in the year as a whole again conceals a change of direction in the course of the year. A rapid expansion in the earlier part of the year was short-lived and soon turned into a stagnation of domestic demand and output which continued into 1971, a year with the lowest growth rate of the post-war period. With the exception of public consumption, all sectors of demand contributed to the recession. Private consumption decelerated sharply, gross fixed-capital formation declined while exports grew no faster than in 1970.

Over-all expansion speeded up only very moderately in 1972 as a whole; but in the third quarter of the year there were indications of the beginning of a renewed upturn. The recession had then lasted for three years, an exceptionally long period not only in Italy's experience but also by comparison with other countries.

The incipient upturn was interrupted by the protracted wage negotiations with the metal-workers' union already mentioned and the widespread labour unrest which reduced industrial production in industries directly or indirectly affected. But, with the conclusion of the wage-round in the spring of 1973, industrial expansion was resumed on a wide front. An upward tendency of demand also became more accentuated in the early part of 1973, consumer expenditure, based on rapid increases in household incomes, being the most dynamic sector. Investment, which like consumption had begun to revive in 1972, was checked again by the labour conflicts and uncertainties about the outcome of wage negotiations. But inquiries into investment intentions in 1973 indicated an expansionary tendency, sparked off by the need to absorb cost increases through rationalization and productivity-raising investments; and there were also indications of a prospective rise in 'capital-widening' investment.

In assessing the prospects for sustained expansion, several notes of caution must be sounded. First in question is the elasticity of supply. Clearly labour supply is no obstacle to further expansion; but the protracted stagnation of investment represents a danger of bottlenecks even though capacities continue to be under-utilized in some sectors.

Another problem area is indicated by the increasing dependence on imports, the less dynamic export growth, and a worsened balance of trade. The very high rate of import growth has reflected both conjunctural and structural factors. Rapidly rising imports of raw materials and investment goods have reflected both price increases and rising domestic demand; but a major negative long-term feature has been the marked deterioration of the food balance already mentioned. A deficit of 570 billion lire in 1965 increased to more than 1,300 billion in 1971 and more than 1,550 billion in 1972 and continued to rise further in 1973. While food consumption, in particular of meat, has increased steadily in recent years, production has tended to decline. The increasing failure of domestic agriculture to meet growing demand has reflected a failure to adapt to new patterns of consumer demand; moreover, social factors and relatively low incomes in agriculture compared with other sectors have led to a depopulation even of the more fertile areas of the countryside, and an inefficient and high-cost distribution system lessens the competitiveness of domestic food supplies.

Exports slowed down sharply in the second half of 1972, due to cost increases and temporary supply limitations caused by the strikes, and they were affected again by the customs strikes in early 1973. While an acceleration of exports could be expected from the *de facto* devaluation of the lira and the expansion of world trade, the loss of impetus of some of the traditional Italian export industries such as textiles and clothing may have been due to more permanent factors.

Other adverse features in mid-1973 were the unprecedented rate of price inflation which surpassed that of all other Common Market countries; the constraint imposed on domestic expansion by a weak balance-of-payments position; and, finally, uncertainty generated by the international currency crisis and the uncertain outlook for the lira parity.

Italian policy-makers are thus faced with a difficult task of reconciling conflicting short-term objectives: providing support to the re-expansion while keeping inflation in check and strengthening the balance of payments, deciding on the lira exchange rate and adhering to Italy's commitments to a joint Common Market policy. Turning to longer-term prospects, there is a growing conviction that a renewed upswing can be sustained without eventual crisis only if the fundamental structural problems of Italian society and institutions are at last tackled with resolution and speed. In this context the Governor of the Bank of Italy recently launched a vigorous attack on the public authorities and their policies, or policy omissions, which created a great stir in Italian public opinion.[3] On the specific issue of the prospects for a sustained economic expansion he stated that a recovery of productive activity which is not accompanied by an efficient use of resources both in public and private sectors risks proving a transitory phenomenon instead of initiating a desirable new phase of development of the Italian economy. We must therefore carefully review the policies pursued in recent years, which were excessively oriented towards the maintenance of existing patterns of resource utilization. They helped to crystallize the *status quo* and provided a kind of public guarantee for maintaining factors of production in low productivity uses. . . . The tendency to protect acquired positions is supported by convergent attitudes of the political classes, entrepreneurs, and trade unions. In this behaviour pattern, legitimate motivations of a social character are mixed up with others—less explicit but no less prevalent—which rally round the defence of privileged positions.

It is an open question whether the new Centro-Sinistra Government which took over in July 1973 will be able to use the bitter experiences of the past for implementing a more forceful and consistent policy of planning and reform. The package of emergency measures taken so far is analysed in the concluding chapter.

Meanwhile, having traced the general trends of development in the last four years, it is now appropriate to look more closely at some of their features.

(iv) WAGES, PRODUCTIVITY, AND UNIT LABOUR COSTS

Wage increases accelerated in 1969 and reached unprecedented proportions in 1970 after the conclusion of the new wage agreements. The rate of increase slowed in 1971 and 1972, but remained substantial even though labour market conditions could certainly not be described as strained.

Although trade-union activity at the national level became much less turbulent after the 1969–70 wage-round, agitation at the enterprise level increased, with demands for wage increases, reductions of the standard working week, improvement of working conditions, and other claims; and there were a number of reasons for rapid wage increases in the absence of over-all labour market pressures—automatic wage adjustments to cost-of-living increases,* the fact that the major collective agreements concluded earlier set the pace for subsequent wage claims even though economic conditions had radically changed, and the existence of pockets of labour shortages even though the non-active population continued to grow (see Part Two).

Wage drift however was not particularly accentuated in the period following the 'hot autumn'. The gap between wage rates and hourly earnings tended to reflect the interplay of the timing of collective bargaining and of bargaining at the enterprise level. With bunching of wage agreements, wage drift diminished after the conclusion of the collective wage bargains and in some branches even became negative. But drift became more marked again in the course of 1971. (For manufacturing, see Table 4.)

The slower growth, or even decline, of productivity up to 1972 was due to a variety of factors: lower capacity utilization, the progressive shortening of the working week, and frequent strikes and absenteeism. Moreover, earlier efforts to raise productivity by intensifying the pace of work in the factory had led to strong resistance against the resulting physical and mental strain on workers; and the reorganization of production processes to meet the demand for improved working conditions now contributed to a slowdown of productivity advances.

But this loss of momentum in the recession appears to have been also part of a longer-term process. A comparison of productivity advances in the private sector during 1964–71 with those during 1958–64 shows a decline from a 6·7 per cent to a 5·6 per cent annual average. Rates of increase fell in agriculture, industry, and tertiary activities alike, though

* Wages are automatically adjusted to increases in the cost of living each quarter if the rise in the cost of living amounts to one point or more. The point increases were: 9 in 1969, 8 in 1970, 9 in 1971, 13 in 1972, and as many as 12 by May 1973. It has been estimated that a one-point adjustment represents an additional labour cost of 60 billion lire a year. The confederation of small and medium-sized industries has calculated that, since January 1972, wages have been increased on average by 17,500 lire by the cost-of-living adjustment—an amount equivalent to increases obtained through wage agreements.

with varying experiences for individual branches within these major sectors. There was some tendency for sectoral rates of growth of productivity to converge, as a combined effect of changes in rates of increase within individual branches of activity and changes in the weights of these branches in total employment and output.

Thus the contribution made to the over-all growth of output per worker by movement from agriculture to other occupations diminished with the reduced weight of agriculture in the economy, and the former rapid rise of agricultural labour productivity itself slackened. In manufacturing, a slow-down of over-all productivity growth from 6·8 per cent to 5·5 per cent a year between the two periods was largely accounted for by a sharply declining contribution of clothing (on account of reductions both of its weight and of its specific productivity growth) and of chemicals (because of the weakening of its own productivity advances alone).[4]

Unit labour costs rose steeply in 1970 and 1971 in manufacturing, in all industry, and in the private sector as a whole. As in other industrial countries, output and productivity increases tend to move more or less in step in the early phases of cyclical downturns or upturns, with productivity falling as capacity is less fully utilized. In Italy, the timing—and bunching—of wage agreements produced steep rises in unit wage costs as output and productivity lost momentum. But with the slowing down of wage increases in 1972 and some shake-out of under-employed labour, which helped to accelerate productivity growth again, the rise of unit labour costs slowed down, though the 1973 concessions may now again have speeded up the rise.

The persistence of cost inflation during the recession can also be attributed in part to structural features of the Italian economy. Differences in levels of output per worker in different branches of activity remain substantial. A 'wage–wage spiral' spread increases conceded in high-productivity branches to low-productivity branches where the impact on unit cost was greater. In sheltered branches of production, including services, cost increases could relatively easily be passed on to prices, and there was little incentive to raise efficiency. Price rises in these sectors were reflected in the cost of living and, through sliding-scale adjustments, again raised costs in many sectors. In this context also, the simultaneity of wage agreements played its role.

Another permanent feature contributing to cost inflation was the lack of occupational mobility of the labour force due to substantial differences in levels of education and professional training and to the absence of a labour market policy with appropriate instruments for adjusting supply to demand. Hence partial bottlenecks developed in some branches, occupations, and qualifications despite unemployment and under-employment in others.

A rather specific cause of high labour costs to enterprises, and of labour unrest, is the particularly large share of employers' contributions to social security funds in total labour costs. The total bill for 'dependent' labour in 1970 was made up of 72 per cent gross pay and 28 per cent social security payments, compared with averages for the Common Market countries of 81 and 19 per cent (West Germany 87 and 13; France 78 and 22 per cent). As a result there was a much wider gap between Italy and other countries with respect to average pay received by workers than with respect to total labour cost, the former representing—it is estimated—72 per cent of the Common Market average and the latter 81 per cent.[5] At the same time the quantity and quality of the services rendered by the social security institutions have certainly been far below those attained in other countries. All this has contributed both to weakening the financial position of enterprises in a recession—and particularly in conditions of slack demand but still rising wages, since social security contributions rise with the wage bill—and to the lingering discontent of Italian workers.

In this context there has been a great deal of discussion about the 'fiscalization' of social security contributions. This measure was proposed as a partial compensation for the rise in direct labour costs and was to help enterprises to reconstitute their savings and hence to undertake new investments. The decision seemed imminent and modalities for its implementation were proposed in various quarters—steps to preserve discrimination in favour of enterprises operating in the South or of small and medium-sized firms, or to ensure that the amounts saved would really be spent on investment. There was also a proposal to finance from the budget any rise in wages, beyond a stated increment, due to the cost-of-living adjustment. However, as has so often been the case in the past, what seemed a burning issue one day receded into the background the next. In the meantime the case for fiscalization to stimulate investment appears to have dwindled since rising prices have raised enterprise profits, at least for the time being. The transfer of social security payments to the budget had also been intended as a structural measure to be linked to the health-service reform and may yet be revived on some unknown day in the future when that long-promised reform becomes reality.

One of the major, and most vehemently criticized, aspects of the inflationary process in Italy is the widespread existence of parasitic incomes, of speculation, and of waste in many activities catering for essential needs. This is shown in the archaic, inefficient, and costly retail-distribution system. Wholesale trade, especially in food, is concentrated in a few hands and operated with often ruthless methods which exploit farmers and reap excessive profits. Another example is the provision of housing, where the scarcity of building areas and the low level of publicly controlled and financed low-cost house-building have encouraged reckless real-estate speculation and pushed up rents and the price for dwellings (see Part Two). In certain liberal professions, especially in the medical profession, there are many instances of excessive fees. The social security institutions are another flagrant example of wasteful and cumbersome operations, with over-staffing, political favouritism, and excessive salaries which explain their high running costs and low standard of services.

(v) PRICE INFLATION

Price increases accelerated in 1969 and, alarmingly, in the latter part of 1972 and the early months of 1973. As the figures below indicate, food and raw-material prices were largely responsible for the exceptionally rapid rise in the general index of wholesale prices. Consumer prices, particularly for food, rose at rates never experienced in Italy in the last twenty years.

Recent price developments
Percentage changes

	Dec. '70– Dec. '71	Dec. '71– Dec. '72	July '72– Dec. '72[1]	Jan. '73– March '73[2]
Wholesale prices				
General index	2·7	7·3	11·2	3·7
Food	3·4	11·0	19·7	3·9
Industrial materials	−2·4	10·3	13·1	10·4
Industrial products	2·9	5·2	7·6	2·1
Consumer prices				
General index	4·7	7·4	9·5	13·2
Food	4·6	8·8	11·5	13·5
Other commodities	4·8	5·3	6·0	11·9
Services	4·6	7·6	9·8	11·3

1. Annual rate.
2. March 1973 over December 1972 at annual rates for consumer prices.
Source: Bank of Italy elaborations on the basis of ISTAT (Institute of Statistics) data, published in *Relazione Annuale* (1972).

In the year 1972 as a whole, import unit values remained relatively stable, when compared with the sharp increases in the preceding years; and this seems to reflect the reluctance in many countries to raise export prices in national currencies after the currency realignments of December 1971, when prices expressed in dollars had already been increased considerably by effective currency revaluations against the dollar. The low level of domestic demand has induced Italian exporters to seek to enlarge the volume of sales rather than to raise export prices more rapidly and, benefiting also from the slight devaluation of the lira at the end of 1971, Italian exports did in fact rise much faster than those of the O.E.C.D. countries as a group. There appears to have been no deterioration in the price-competitiveness of Italian exports in 1972 as a whole or in the immediately preceding years.

More recently, a combination of external and domestic factors has contributed to the price explosion. Externally, there was the synchronization of inflation in various countries of western Europe, where a rapid growth of demand has come up against supply limitations, and a sharp rise in world prices of industrial raw materials and foods.

On the domestic front there was, apart from the rise in unit labour costs and the structural cost-raising factors already referred to, a shortage of some foods, particularly meat, which was due both to long-term factors and to a bad agricultural year.* In addition, the introduction on 1 January 1973 of the value-added tax led to price increases both in anticipation of the tax and as its aftermath. And there was, finally, the impact of the *de facto* devaluation of the lira.

Some of these factors might have been expected to have only a once-for-all effect. However, a cumulative process has set in as inflationary expectations, reinforced by recent signs of an upturn, asserted themselves. Moreover, since rapid price increases have become an international phenomenon, international competition no longer appears the obstacle that it formerly was to passing on cost increases.

Since price inflation accelerated in conditions of stagnation and rising unemployment or, more recently, of a rather vulnerable upturn, over-all restrictive measures seem neither desirable nor very likely to check the cost-inflation process.

In these circumstances the authorities took little or no

* Increases in food prices have a more important impact on the cost of living in Italy than elsewhere since the share of household incomes spent on food is still higher here than in other industrial countries.

action on the price front until July–August 1973 when measures to check price increases were adopted by the new Centro-Sinistra Government as part of a policy programme to deal with an emergency situation.

(vi) PRIVATE CONSUMPTION

The rate of change of private consumption has fluctuated considerably during the last cycle. Expenditure at constant prices increased fairly rapidly in 1969, accelerated to a rate of 8 per cent—the highest since 1963—in 1970 but rose by only 2·8 and 3·8 per cent in 1971 and 1972. Accounting as it did for 64 per cent of GNP, the sharp deceleration of private consumption was an important factor in the recession.

The behaviour of private consumption was in apparent contradiction with the large shift of income distribution in favour of wages and salaries. The share of income from employment in total national income rose from 59 per cent in 1970 to 62·4 per cent in 1971 and retained that share in 1972. But while disposable household income rose by 11·2 per cent from 1970 to 1971, private consumption rose (at current prices) by only 8·2 per cent and the annual increase of household savings accelerated from 4·5 per cent between 1969 and 1970 to 27·2 per cent in the following year.

The apparent sharp reduction in the propensity to consume can be attributed to a variety of causes connected with the recession. Uncertain employment and income prospects probably accounted for some increase in precautionary savings. Another factor was the partial elimination from employment of low-income groups with a particularly high propensity to consume. A longer-term feature in the unexpected behaviour of consumer demand may have been a slower rise over a number of earlier years of the stock of financial assets held by households and the desire to restore a more balanced relationship between these and current consumer expenditure.

In the second half of 1972 and the early part of 1973 there was a return to a more 'normal' relationship between disposable income and consumer expenditure. For the whole of 1972 both rose by 10 per cent at current prices, and in volume terms private consumption accelerated despite substantial increases in consumer prices.

In a longer-term view, it must be noted that Italy devoted 64 per cent of GNP to private consumption in 1971, a higher share than in any other Common Market country. On the other hand, *per capita* consumers' expenditure in absolute terms is still well below that of other highly developed countries even though the gap has been narrowing. It is estimated to fall short of *per capita* consumption in the Netherlands by 15 per cent, in the United Kingdom by 27 per cent, and in Germany, France, and Denmark by more than one-third. A continuation of the tendency to close the gap may be considered a positive factor in that it provides support to economic expansion; but if only more skilful demand management could change the pattern of aggregate expenditure and economic growth, productive investment and urgently needed social expenditures would today have a prior claim.

(vii) THE STAGNATION OF INVESTMENT

In Italy the need for a high rate and steady expansion of investment is perhaps more pressing than in most other industrial countries of western Europe. Additional jobs have to be created to absorb a labour potential which is much larger than official unemployment and under-employment figures indicate; alternative employment opportunities need to be provided for the overcrowded low-productivity sectors, particularly in the South. The lack of adequate economic and social infra-structure calls for large investments. In the advanced industrial sector, confronted with sharp labour-cost increases and international competition, productivity-raising investment cannot safely be forgone and the backward sectors eventually have to modernize and rationalize their production processes in order to survive.

But gross fixed-capital formation returned to its 1963 peak

level only in 1967, marked some progress in 1968 and early 1969, then declined sharply in the last quarter of 1969 and, after a brief recovery in 1970, fell again in the next two years. Its share in GNP has fallen from 22·5 per cent in 1961–2 to 18·8 per cent in 1971–2. Inadequate domestic investment and an accelerating fall in employment, with capital exports, are among the most disturbing features of recent economic trends.

But the various components of total fixed investment have in fact moved differently in the latest recession (Table 2). Residential construction had the strongest deflationary impact, because of the size of its decline in 1970 and 1971, its weight in total fixed investment, and the repercussions on industries supplying the building sector; and the reasons for its sharp drop were connected with legislative and administrative measures taken in anticipation of a housing reform. A 1967 law—the so-called 'legge ponte'—reduced the areas exempt from limitations on residential construction. It required building licences for the whole of communal areas, in anticipation of the preparation of detailed town-plans. The licences issued during an interim period from 31 August 1967 to 1 September 1968 could not be extended, and authorized constructions had to be completed within two years of their being started. This produced an artificial building boom in 1968 and 1969. The subsequent decline and the only very modest increase in 1972 were due to a combination of complex factors which will be discussed in Part Two.

Investment in machinery and equipment expanded rapidly in 1970, largely as a result of a catching up in the earlier part of the year on projects interrupted or delayed during the strikes; but subsequently it stagnated or declined.

A feature of particular interest was the divergent investment behaviour of the private and public enterprise sector. While private business investment declined sharply, outlays by public corporations continued to rise rapidly, in contrast with the simultaneous downturn of the two sectors' investment expenditures in the earlier recession and the more prolonged slump in the public than in the private enterprise sector (see Fig. 3).

Looking at a longer period, the share of public enterprise investment in total enterprise investment rose from 19 per cent in 1961 to 49 per cent in 1972. This enormous shift has important policy implications which will be commented upon in due course.

The protracted investment crisis in the private sector has been due to a number of partly inter-related causes. Stagnation of production and the rises in unit costs (labour costs and costs of imported inputs) already described, and—in branches of activity exposed to foreign competition—difficulty in raising prices in line with costs, produced a squeeze on both total profits and profit margins. The share of profits in total value added in manufacturing industry (including profits of public corporations, which have fallen even more than those of large private enterprises) reached its lowest level of the whole post-war period in 1971 (see Table 4). Moreover, the slow rate of expansion of aggregate demand and output, on the one hand, and the uncertain outcome of the wage negotiations accompanied by new strike waves at the turn of 1972, on the other, made for depressed expectations.

But in the latter part of 1972 private industry's investment demand began to pick up as industrial production revived, capacity utilization improved, and inflationary conditions abroad rendered price increases easier.* Information supplied by branches of the Bank of Italy now suggests that important investment programmes have been planned, though these appear to aim mainly at readjusting production processes to the norms of the new labour contracts and are expected to create little additional employment.

* A Bank of Italy sample inquiry covering 423 manufacturing companies showed gross profits declining by 30 per cent from 1968 to 1971 and net profits of 267 billion lire turning into net losses of 154 billion (*Relazione Annuale*, 1972). A later survey of 134 manufacturing companies showed gross profits rising by 15 per cent from 1971 to 1972 and net losses falling from 89 billion to 72 billion lire.

(viii) THE FINANCING OF ENTERPRISE INVESTMENT

Special difficulties have arisen in recent years in the financing of private business investment. The change in income distribution in favour of wages and salaries, already mentioned, has been accompanied by a fall in the shares of independent traders and of corporate retained profits (including those of public corporations) in national income (Table 5); and within the total saving generated in the private sector of the economy, there has been a marked change in the pattern—a much larger share than in the past being contributed by 'households' as compared with 'corporations'. Self-financing of enterprise investment has thus become more difficult. For the sample of 423 companies mentioned above, the share of gross investment self-financed fell from a maximum of 80 per cent in 1968 to 26 per cent in 1971, and the corresponding net financing ratios were 37 and 13 per cent.

But 'The period of the economic miracle had created the myth—which it was difficult to dispel—that self-financing was essential for a high rate of investment.'[6] In fact, the shrinking of enterprise saving need not, of itself, put unsurmountable obstacles in the way of financing an expansion of investment (though lower profits may well reduce the desire to invest). External financing does, however, depend upon an efficient mechanism for channelling saving by other sectors of the economy to productive investment.

External finance can be supplied by risk-capital or by fixed-interest lending. But access to risk-capital is rendered difficult in Italy through the lack of appropriate capital market institutions and the reluctance of both individual and institutional savers to invest in shares.

Moreover, fiscal treatment and other provisions render financing through share issues disadvantageous both for the issuer and the buyer of shares. The obligatory registration of share ownership has a strong psychological impact; the high cost of issue (amounting to about double one year's dividends) is another discouragement. In addition the system of taxation of corporations and of unincorporated businesses has been highly complex. First, they are taxed on total income. In addition, all enterprises are subject to a corporation tax which has two components, a tax on paid-up capital plus reserves and another on net profits in excess of 6 per cent of the value of taxable assets. Distributed profits are then taxed again under the progressive personal income tax.

The distribution of financial assets held by households, at the end of 1971

	percentage
Cash	8·1
Bank deposits	38·0
Other deposits	11·1
Fixed income securities	18·6
Shares	6·5
Mathematical reserves[1]	8·4
Foreign assets	9·3
Total	101·0

1. Reserves held by insurance companies against households' policies.
Source: Bank of Italy, *Relazione Annuale* (1972).

A reform of joint-stock companies has been under discussion for many years. Its purpose was to render investment in shares more attractive to household savers, and the relevant provisions are the creation of savings shares without obligatory registration, more favourable tax treatment of these shares, and a guaranteed minimum dividend; company balance sheets which have been highly obscure were to be given greater clarity and institutions were to be created to control company accounts and to disseminate information on company operations. This is another reform proposal which has failed to be implemented so far.

The public has always shown a preference for investing in fixed income 'bearer' securities. The bond market is, however, largely dominated by the public or publicly controlled sector and the special credit institutions. Tax provisions discriminate against privately issued bonds, whose yield is taxed at 35–6 per cent, while public bonds are entirely tax-free and those issued by the special credit institutions are subject to a very low tax.

There has therefore been a long-term tendency for enterprises to increase indebtedness to financial intermediaries, mainly the special credit institutions, firstly because the cost of borrowing is much lower than that of raising funds in the capital market, and also because the liberal and often indiscriminate granting of subsidized credit is legally tied to recourse to borrowing.

The average composition of the increase in external finance of enterprises in the period 1964–71

	percentage
Short-term indebtedness	35·0
Medium- and long-term loans	37·4
Of which special credit institutions	26·0
Bonds	9·9
Shares and equity participations	17·7
Total	100·0

Source: Bank of Italy, *Relazione Annuale* (1972)

From a special Bank of Italy investigation it appears that for a group of 200 large enterprises the share of indebtedness in total liabilities has rapidly increased (from 36 per cent in 1958 to 43 per cent in 1963 and to 47 per cent in 1970), not only during periods of substantial investment expansion but also when investment slowed down or stagnated.

In the recession, a level of indebtedness which was already high at the outset, together with difficult access to risk-capital and the decline in self-financing, meant that further borrowing constituted a threat to the financial balance of the enterprise. With the deterioration of the financial structure, access to risk-capital as well as to credit became more costly and these conditions forced a number of enterprises into insolvency, recourse to government assistance, or selling out to foreign companies or to public corporations.

As tends to be the case in other industrial countries in similar circumstances, small and medium-sized enterprises suffered from such difficulties more than the large ones, and the former group are still very important in Italy. In 1969, 45 per cent of employment in manufacturing was in establishments with less than 50 workers, and in the South alone as much as 64 per cent;* and the self-financing ratio in this group has been considerably below that of the larger enterprises. In a sample of 399 private manufacturing firms the self-financing ratio during 1961–9 averaged 59 per cent whereas for the larger companies it was 82 per cent.[7] The need for the smaller enterprises to rely on external finance was thus greater even in good times, and they were all the more vulnerable in a recession. This was not only because the share of indebtedness in their total financing had been greater at the outset but also because more stringent conditions are applied to the granting of credit (and to the concession of subsidized loans) to small, medium-sized, and new firms than to the well-known, established, and large ones. The discrimination against the smaller enterprises is reflected in a steep decline during periods of credit restraint in the share of credits of less than 1 billion lire in the total credits granted. When monetary policy was expansionary, the decline in interest rates was steeper for credits to large companies.[8]

In a broader context, the conclusion to be derived from the financing pattern of Italian enterprises is that their heavy dependence on borrowing from banks and special credit institutions, together with the Government's excessive reliance on monetary policy for demand management, has serious implications for the achievement of a high and steady rate of investment expansion. The impact of monetary restraint, to restore balance-of-payments equilibrium and/or relative price stability, falls particularly heavily on investment in these circumstances. Moreover, the institutional weaknesses of the domestic capital market could also be

* 28 per cent of the labour force is employed in enterprises with less than 10 employees compared with 19 per cent in France and 13 per cent in Germany.

partly responsible for the large flow of funds abroad, which complicates the balance-of-payments problem.

(ix) THE MANAGERIAL PROBLEM

In addition to the factors reviewed above, the present industrial difficulties also owe something to a managerial crisis. During the recovery from the 1964–5 recession there was as yet little awareness of a permanent change in the industrial environment, and of the fact that the easy period of industrial expansion based on low, and relatively slowly rising, wages had come to an end for ever; and industrial management has been slow to adapt to the trade unions' assertion of their newly acquired power. Government attitudes to management in the growing public sector of industry have also been inappropriate. In a wider context, there has been a widespread reluctance among the managerial class to break with individualistic attitudes and develop a sense of responsibility towards the economic and social problems of the country.

In large areas of industry there survived in smaller enterprises a type of dynastic family ownership with traditional, autocratic, and outdated methods of management. The 'captains of industry' were often opposed to organizational innovation and rigid in their attitudes towards their employees, as well as hostile to State intervention and generally mistrustful of Centro-Sinistra Governments. There was further a growing 'senility of the entrepreneurial class', as owners of firms refused to hand over their power to the younger generation.

Some of the large companies were run by financial groups, rather than by professional and expert industrial managers, resulting in frequent mis-timing of investment decisions and many instances of a misallocation of investment resources. The liberal and insufficiently selective granting of special investment incentives gave further support to a wasteful use of investment finance.

The lack of adequate control over the use of public funds

by public corporations and the manner of recruitment of managers for the public enterprise sector have also played a role in the deterioration of managerial efficiency (see Part Two).

Another factor in the emergence of a fundamental weakness in the Italian industrial structure was the ageing of the capital stock built up during the investment boom and the slowing down of technical progress just at a time when wage increases accelerated. Technical innovations have been based largely on imported and adapted technologies and resources devoted to research and development have been exceptionally limited in Italy compared with other industrial countries. Thus research and development expenditure represented 0·7 per cent of GNP in 1969 compared with 2·3 per cent in the United Kingdom and France, 1·7 per cent in Germany, and 3·1 per cent in the United States.

Recently there have been encouraging signs in some private industrial circles of profound changes in attitudes. The most significant were perhaps the statements made by Giovanni and Umberto Agnelli of Fiat, who are among the most influential and progressive leaders of Italian industry. Their pronouncements, on the new role of the entrepreneur in Italian society and the need to adapt enterprise structure and organization to a new model of development, have aroused considerable interest. They argue for social efficiency rather than solely profitability as the major concern of industrial management, and for a frank dialogue between the modern manager and the trade unions, and relations of partnership rather than antagonism with the workers' representatives. Private industry must show its readiness to co-operate with all its social partners—workers' organizations, the government, and public corporations—in the achievement of common aims. The industrial world must fill the vacuum left by political power in the promotion of reforms.[9]

There have also been more frequent public confrontations than in the past, between heads of industry, trade-union bosses, the academic world, and political and party chiefs, on the steps to be taken to overcome the recent industrial crisis. The opposing factions and interests appear to be approaching a consensus both on the diagnosis of the ills from which Italy is suffering and on the cures to be adopted. This would have been unthinkable only a short time ago.

Another sign of a new wind blowing is the growing turbulence within Confindustria (the Italian Confederation of Industry). After a first attack some time ago on the 'establishment' of Confindustria, its structure, organization, and policies, by one of its members, Mr. Leopoldo Pirelli, there followed another highly critical appraisal in a document by Umberto Agnelli which appeared towards the end of 1972. It contained proposals for a new industrial policy and asked for a reform of Confindustria in the direction of wider participation by the industrial world, both in Confindustria activities and in the problems of the country. It accused the confederation of excessive isolation, centralization, and rigidity. It had not lived up to the expectations of its members in proposing and pursuing solutions for the recent difficulties and it neglected the particular problems of the numerous small enterprises. While there is much opposition within the ranks of Confindustria to proposals for a more active and responsible social role, these proposals are supported by many young industrialists and continue to be discussed and developed.

CHAPTER 3

BUDGETARY AND MONETARY POLICY

(i) THE BUDGETARY INSTRUMENT

An efficient and flexible budget instrument, operating in co-ordination with monetary policy, is of particular importance in Italy where three major policy objectives have to be pursued simultaneously: the achievement and maintenance of a rate of expansion sufficient to make full use of the growth potential of the economy; the countering of any spontaneous tendencies for cyclical fluctuations in demand and output; and the reconciliation of these objectives with the longer-term aim of structural change, in particular of narrowing the gap between the Centre–North and the South of the country and of shifting resources from private to social use.

In the past budgetary policy has, on the whole, contributed little to the achievement of any of these aims, and demand-management policies have had to rely largely on monetary instruments to maintain—and attempt to reconcile—internal or external balance. Restraint of demand by any means must involve risk of short-term loss of output and employment; but, as has been explained, restrictive policies in Italy have tended to bear particularly heavily on investment demand, which has responded only slowly to monetary stimulus in expansionary phases of policy. Had more effective budgetary and fiscal instruments been available, it might have been possible to concentrate restriction more on private and public consumption—doubtless with some secondary effects on investment demand but with a possibility of less long-term loss of productive capacity—and to reinforce more effectively any monetary stimulus.

In fact, short-term demand management has involved

unsatisfactory compromises between objectives that were conflicting (given the measures available), and very little progress has been achieved in speeding up some urgently needed structural transformations of the economy.

Since 1965, budgetary policy has been used more deliberately than before, but its over-all influence has often been inappropriate to the needs of the economy. In both 1967 and 1970, when stimulus would have been appropriate, the budgetary influence was either restrictive or negligible (see Fig. 5). In the inflationary conditions of 1963 the budget was expansionist when monetary policy had turned restrictive. The budgetary influence was positive again, and this time rightly, in 1965, 1971, and 1972; but, particularly in the latter years, the expansionary impact was insufficient.* The timing of reversals of policy was hesitant, and decisions were frequently so much delayed that their impact came at a time when an opposite influence would have been appropriate; and even when the budget influenced aggregate demand in the right direction, the main expansion (or contraction) was often in components of demand which were inappropriate to longer-term objectives.

In the three years 1970–2, general government net indebtedness rose from some 1,328 billion lire to 2,644 billion and 4,456 billion; thus it first doubled in a year and then rose by over 80 per cent, and the 1973 deficit is estimated at double that of 1972. But the increases in total expenditure have been largely, or more than, accounted for by current expenditure rather than by investment outlays. Thus, while current outlays increased by 3,488 billion lire from 1970 to 1971 and by 4,123 billion from 1971 to 1972, the corresponding increases in general government investment were only 90 billion and 376 billion respectively (see Table 9). Such increases in current expenditure, which consisted

* The impact of the various items of general government revenue and expenditure and of the total budget on GNP has been calculated by the Bank of Italy on the basis of the Hansen model which estimates the multiplier effects of changes in various budget components. See the O.E.C.D. publications quoted in Chapter 3, note 1.

mainly of wages and salaries and transfer payments, have the defect of imparting greater rigidity to future budgets since a large part of them is irreversible. An expansion of current expenditure has, moreover, a much smaller multiplier effect than a similar increase in public investment would have.

There are several basic reasons for the ineffectiveness of budgetary policy. First is the structure of the budget; second, the procedural, institutional, and administrative framework within which budgetary policy is formulated and implemented; and finally antiquated and over-cautious attitudes towards deliberately using budget deficits as a policy measure to induce expansion.

Budget components

The composition of the budget has changed considerably over the last twenty years, and in directions which reduce the efficiency of budgetary policy in several important respects. The share of total current expenditure in GNP has increased from 22 per cent in 1951–2 to 36 per cent in 1971–2 (see Table 10); and during the same period the share of general government investment in GNP stagnated at a very low level. The share in GNP of government current expenditure on goods and services increased moderately, but the ratio of current subsidies and transfers to GNP more than doubled. These shifts reduced the contribution that expenditure changes make both to demand management and to the achievement of longer-term objectives. The multiplier effect of transfers is smaller than that of public investment, or even public consumption, while the much more rapid rise of the last category compared with that of general government investment worked in the same direction.

The share of current government revenue in GNP rose less than that of current expenditure. Within the total, the share of tax receipts rose from 15 to 18 per cent. The direct tax ratio rose gradually to close to 7 per cent while that of indirect taxation declined somewhat between 1961–2 and 1971–2, though still remaining nearly double the direct tax ratio. The most dynamic items in current revenue were social security payments to social welfare institutions, mainly made by employers. Their share in GNP more than doubled, and they have contributed slightly more than indirect taxes to current government revenue in recent years. The implications of the revenue structure are that fiscal policy has had to rely mainly on indirect taxes and social security contributions for influencing demand, since variations in the small volume of direct taxation could not be expected to have an important impact.

In international comparison of shares of government revenues in GNP, Italy ranks very low among the industrial countries of western Europe, and the composition of its revenue is very different from that of other countries, except for France.[2]

If social security contributions are included, the Italian tax ratio ranked thirteenth among all European countries in 1968–70 with a share of 30 per cent of GNP compared with 43 per cent in Sweden, 40 per cent in the Netherlands, 37 per cent in the United Kingdom, 36 per cent in France, and 34 per cent in Germany. If social security payments are excluded, Italy moves down to the eighteenth place. The share of indirect taxation in total taxation was higher in Italy than in any of the major industrial countries; for social security payments, Italy topped the list with the exception of France; the share of direct taxation was correspondingly low at 18 per cent of total tax receipts, compared with 39 per cent in the United Kingdom. These substantial differences in the budget structure have important consequences, not only for the comparative efficiency of fiscal instruments for demand management and structural purposes but also for the integration of Italy's tax structure with other Common Market countries.

The change in the significance of major budgetary components in the whole economy has perhaps even more serious implications for the achievement of longer-term objectives than it has for stabilization policies. Thus the share of public consumption in GNP has shown a long-term tendency to decline; it represented over 16 per cent of GNP in 1951–2, a little more than 13 per cent in 1961–2 and only 12 per cent in 1971–2. The share of general government investment represents a mere 2·5 per cent of GNP. The importance of social expenditures (civil public consumption and social investment) has decreased. By contrast the share of transfers to the private sector rose sharply, with a long-term stimulating effect on private consumption, in the last decade. We are thus witnessing an increasing importance of the private sector in determining the uses of GNP, which is in flagrant contradiction to the proclaimed fundamental aims of the authorities.

Institutional, administrative, and procedural obstacles

Nevertheless, as in all other modern industrial countries of western Europe, the size and functions of the public sector have enormously increased in the post-war period. But in Italy the institutions of public financing and administration have remained antiquated and inefficient and ill-adapted to take on new tasks. The division of power between the main decision centres of economic policy within the government sector is excessive; and public institutions and 'parallel bureaucracies' have proliferated without any clear delimitation of functions. The multiplicity of uncoordinated parts in the government machine has produced confusion, uncertainty, and excessive delays in getting things done. These weaknesses have been accentuated by political instability and frequent changes of government. They have been a major obstacle to the formulation and implementation of efficient stabilization policies as well as to the use of public expenditures to pursue medium-term economic objectives. An elimination of these basic deficiencies probably depends upon a reform of the whole public administration, which has been a recurrent theme in political and economic discussions for some time.

The heavy and sluggish machinery of Government and administration has made for particularly long lags in each of the three stages of the decision-making process: the assessment of the significance of changes in economic indicators which call for remedial action; the decisions at government and parliamentary level to take action (and on what kind of action to take); the legislative process to authorize such action. Delays then occur in the execution of the decision at the administrative level.

The budget system

Despite some reforms aiming to improve the methods of budget preparation and presentation, the existing budget system does not lend itself to efficient policy-making. The budget is presented on an 'appropriation' basis—estimated receipts and appropriations; and simultaneously an account of arrears of receipts and expenditures from the previous budget year is also submitted. Accounts of cash receipts and disbursements (and more recently, estimates of receipts and expenditures on a national accounts basis) are only prepared and presented *ex post*.

The central government budget is not comprehensive. Excluded from it are the operations of autonomous public institutions and enterprises (apart from the public funds which assist in the financing of their investment) and operations of social security institutions except for transfers to them from the central budget.

The system of direct taxation is extremely complicated, the collection lags very long and tax evasion on a large scale is an acknowledged practice; the tradition of mistrust of the fiscal authorities and the belief that evasion is not a dishonourable act have strong historical roots. 'It must not be forgotten that Milan which is considered the "moral" capital of Italy and which has contributed more than any other city to shape the ethics of the Italian businessman . . . was some hundred years ago the capital of a region subject to an authoritarian foreign government . . . Those from Rome are not more popular than those from Vienna used to be.'[3] There are also innumerable exemptions and provisions for special treatment, and all this makes estimates of current revenue highly uncertain. On the positive side there is the possibility, in principle, of quick variation, and collection, of the broadly-based indirect taxes and of social security contributions. In practice, however, while the Government can decree tax changes, the decrees must simultaneously be presented to Parliament for conversion into laws. If these laws are not voted within 60 days, the decrees lapse automatically. This procedure has frequently prevented urgent measures from being taken in time.

Local government largely relies on taxes and shares of central government revenue which fluctuate with the level of activity; and local government expenditures have therefore tended to follow the cycle.

In the phase of budget preparation, political forces, various Ministerial administrations, and organizations directly concerned with public expenditure projects, all exercise their influence and the budget thus becomes the result of multiple pressures rather than of co-ordinated overall policy decisions. Although there is no explicit stipulation that the aim is a balanced budget, opposition to the idea of deliberately increasing a budget deficit to stimulate the economy persists among the public authorities. In the past, it appears that governments tended to spend in step with such revenues as materialized. When budget deficits occurred or were increased, these were the outcome of unchecked departmental pressures rather than of deliberate policy action.

For the budget to carry out its functions—of short-term demand management and longer-term influence of the economic structure—in an efficient manner, 'a radical transformation of its structure and methods would be required. It is now reduced to a passive instrument which registers impulses, whether external or internal to the administration, and legislation for expenditures which lie beyond any serious control of their compatibility with each other or with planning objectives.'[4]

An important step towards changing budget procedures, so as to give more realistic advance information on estimated revenues and expenditures during the budget period, was the presentation to Parliament of a forecast of central government cash operations in the draft budget for 1972. This related both to new appropriations and to the liquidation of residuals outstanding at the beginning of the year. In addition, it is expected that periodic adjustments of cash budget forecasts will be made during the year, especially in connection with decisions on more important changes in revenue and expenditure, and that analytical information on the operation of other sectors of the public administration will be published.

The flexibility of public expenditure

The scope for varying public expenditure is rather limited in all countries. In Italy current expenditure has been expanding more or less continuously. Transfer payments are difficult to compress, both because they largely depend on irreversible prior commitments and because they are considered socially desirable. Their increases, as well as those of public salaries, could have been better timed to fit in with short-term stabilization objectives. But when the situation has called for a speeding up of the rate of increase of current expenditure, the fear of irreversibility has often prevented such a decision.

As to public investment, it may be considered undesirable to slow down this category of expenditure in times of excess demand pressures in view of the importance of the long-term needs it is intended to meet. Moreover, the interruption of investment projects under way can be a costly procedure.

Both categories of public expenditure, but in particular public investment, are rendered even less flexible in Italy than in other countries because of the institutional and administrative characteristics outlined above. Moreover, a large portion of expenditure has already been decided upon by individual expenditure laws. The flexible part has been estimated to range between only 10 and 15 per cent of the total.

Some evidence of the delays in central government expenditure has been presented in a study on the short-term control of the economy which compares appropriations with cash results.[5] It appears that the appropriations on capital account have almost always exceeded—and for some categories substantially exceeded—outlays, with a tendency for the gap to widen after 1959. More specific evidence in the document on the Italian planning experience already referred to,[6] shows enormous time-lags between the passing of a law authorizing a project and the preparation of the operational details of the project, and another long period before it is finally carried out. Thus, after approval of a law on a school-building programme in July 1967, its preparation went through the following phases: regional committees were invited to submit their proposals; the central committee then collected various data on needs for new schools; in the next round the financial requirements of the regions were estimated; the project was finally approved in January 1970. The preparatory phase thus took two and a half years from the passing of the law. For a project involving elimination of sub-standard housing, four years elapsed between the approval of legislation and the completion of the project. The corresponding lag for some hospital and health assistance projects was more than forty months and for a programme of provincial roads from six to eight years!

Added to such extraordinary delays in carrying out an investment project, once it has been decided upon by law, was the drawback of finance being raised much before any disbursements actually took place, so that the initial impact of such an investment programme could even have been deflationary.

A related problem which is specific to Italian budgets is the large volume of unspent appropriations ('residui passivi'). It derives both from the system of an appropriation budget and from the long delays in carrying out the authorized expenditures. The accumulation of unspent appropriations means that the budget as presented at the beginning of the fiscal year cannot indicate the economic impact it is going to have, and that the intentions of budgetary policy are far from being fully reflected in the budget outcome.

The budgetary system distinguishes between residuals of appropriations ('residui di competenza') and 'residuals proper'. The former represent sums budgeted which have not even led to firm commitments for future expenditure (such as contracts with building firms). Such residuals on capital account can, in principle, be carried forward to subsequent budgets for no more than five years; but residuals proper (those investment projects for which actual commitments have been made) continue to figure in the budget indefinitely, that is until their liquidation.

The following figures give an indication of the dimensions of unspent appropriations. They amounted to 6·9 billion lire in 1969, 7·8 billion in 1970, and 8·7 billion in 1971. Relating unspent appropriations at the end of the budget year (new residuals together with those accumulated in the past) to total expenditure budgeted for that year *plus* the unspent amounts at the beginning of the year, their share was over 35 per cent in 1969, 37 per cent in 1970, and 35 per cent again in 1971. At the end of 1971, 42 per cent of the unspent appropriations related to current expenditure and 58 per cent to capital expenditure, the latter almost entirely a result of unspent investment appropriations. Of the total of newly accrued residuals, the 'appropriation residuals' accounted for 36 per cent in 1970 and for 32 per cent in 1971.[7]

The growth of unspent appropriations was due to a great increase in the number of tasks of the central government administration, an increase which has not been accompanied by improved budget procedures; and more recently unspent appropriations have been connected with the formulation of vast development programmes. The decline in 1971 in the share of the appropriation residuals reflects an effort to speed up and simplify administrative processes, but also the fact that large programmes started during earlier budget periods had got under way.

The fiscal reform

A major fiscal reform had been under discussion for some years, was finally approved in October 1971, and was supposed to be enacted on 1 January 1972. However, the introduction of the new tax system was in fact postponed and divided into two consecutive phases: the new system of indirect taxation was introduced on 1 January 1973 and the reform of direct taxation is to be put into effect in 1974.

The replacement of a general turnover tax and a number of other indirect taxes by a unique value-added tax (V.A.T.) is, of course, one step in the harmonization of tax systems within the Common Market. The general turnover tax was a cascade tax, on the full value of goods and services sold, at every stage of production and distribution and made for variations from sector to sector and from enterprise to enterprise, according to its financial and commercial structure and the degree of its integration. Among the advantages of V.A.T., therefore, are neutrality with respect to international trade and to internal competition, ensuring equal fiscal treatment of every enterprise whatever the number of stages in the production and distribution process. Evasion is more difficult, since every tax-payer depends on his business partners to make correct tax declarations; and price formation is more easily assessed since the share of price due to the tax is singled out. The three V.A.T. rates fixed—which are to be reached by gradual steps—are 6 per cent for food and other essentials, 18 per cent for luxury goods, and 12 per cent for all other goods and services.

The introduction of V.A.T. has had a certain price-raising effect in that, where the tax rates are now lower than before, prices are not being reduced whereas, where they are higher, prices are being raised. The introduction of V.A.T. was accompanied by a great deal of agitation, inadequate preparation, both of the tax collectors and the public, and the improvisation which is customary in Italian procedures, creating a somewhat hysterical climate. Prices were thus often raised far beyond what might be considered a 'normal' consequence of the new tax, in order to profit from the confusion and the public's ignorance—and were sometimes raised in anticipation. Moreover, V.A.T. was introduced at a time of considerable inflationary pressure, and producers and traders attempted partially to compensate for increases in wage and raw-material costs while using V.A.T. as justification. Price increases have consequently exceeded by far those experienced in other countries in connection with the introduction of V.A.T.

The reform of direct taxation was intended to do away with an outdated and highly complicated system comprising a multiplicity of taxes, surtaxes, and supplementary taxes. These had been conceived and added to in a rather haphazard manner as expenditures grew and, with an equal profusion of exemptions and authorized deductions, rendered the tax system so complex that it was difficult either for the tax-payer to understand his liabilities or for the authorities to foresee the revenue changes likely to arise from any given tax change. For taxes raised at the source—taxes on income from employment and social security contributions—there was no lag in collection. For other taxes, the average collection lag was between nineteen and twenty-five months.

The reform aims to impart clarity, simplicity, flexibility, and progressiveness to the tax system, to render it more equitable and evasion more difficult. The new taxes will consist of a single and progressive personal income tax, a tax on income from capital and on capital gains from real estate, and a tax on inheritance and donations. The local authorities will assist in the assessment of these taxes. To reduce the discrimination against private bond issues on the capital market, the disparity between the fiscal treatment applying to issues by private enterprises, public corporations, and special credit institutions is to be narrowed. Other innovations are a centralized and computerized tax register and a clause authorizing the Government to alter rates without prior Parliamentary approval.

It is not possible to anticipate whether the reform will change the share of direct taxes in total revenue. But the new system should make fiscal policy a more efficient policy instrument. It should be easier to forecast receipts and—with evasion reduced—to ensure greater equality of tax treatment of income from employment and other incomes. The speeding up of tax assessment and collection and the greater flexibility of rates are further steps in the right direction. The detailed decrees on direct taxation have been approved at the end of September 1973. The new legislation is considered by many as a point of departure rather than a goal achieved since it still suffers from a number of gaps and anomalies. Moreover, it does not of itself guarantee effective application of the reform. This requires more precise methods of assessment, a new administrative discipline, and a new attitude on the part of tax-payers. All these will take time to achieve; and the obstacles to varying the rate and composition of public expenditure remain.

Proposals for an improvement of the budget instrument

A number of proposals have been put forward for an improvement of the budget as an instrument for both stabilization policies and medium-term planning. The most authoritative among them have been formulated by the Secretary-General of Economic Planning, on the basis of his lengthy inside-experience of the obstacles which the deficiencies of budgetary instruments put in the way both of planning activities and of linking short-term policies with longer-term objectives.[8]

They can be summarized as follows. Even though the tax burden in Italy is light compared with other countries, it cannot be expected that the whole of the increase in resources to be devoted to social infra-structures and the provision of essential services can be met entirely by increasing taxation. Public savings must therefore also be increased through a limitation and rationalization of those expenditures, above all of current expenditure, which involve waste of public funds and do not serve high-priority needs. One means, among others, to achieve such a change would be selective action on transfer payments from the budget so as to limit those going to higher-income groups.

To render the direct tax system itself progressive not only on paper but in reality, numerous unjustified exemptions and alleviations would have to be eliminated. But indirect taxes will remain the most important source of revenue. They could be made more flexible by varying tax rates uniformly or by shifting different categories of goods and services from one tax bracket to another. A limitation of transfer payments should be accompanied by the direct provision of social services by the public sector.

Within the medium-term development plans, programmes should be defined whose execution can be accelerated or slowed down as required by short-run demand-management objectives. In this context other experts also proposed to use the unspent appropriations for rendering expenditure more flexible. The administrative procedures required for using these appropriations are much shorter than for the approval of new investment projects. Thus a list of reserve projects, expenditure for which has already been approved, could be drawn up together with a list of priorities for their use in accelerating or slowing down public expenditure.

(ii) MONETARY POLICY

The weakness of the budgetary instrument, and most other instruments of economic policy, has compelled the Italian authorities to place an almost exclusive reliance on monetary weapons for demand management in the post-war period.

The monetary institutions and instruments are sufficiently powerful for the authorities to exercise a far-reaching control of the monetary and credit system, and the Central Bank also has an exceptionally strong influence on policy.

> The inventiveness of the central banker has been reflected in a continual refinement of the techniques of intervention: new instruments were applied and experimented with . . . for the purpose of widening the margin of manoeuvre of the authorities and for adapting it to changes in the international setting within which the economic system operates.[9]

In particular, a system of industrial credit was built up which

> for its amplitude, the capacity to transform private savings into medium- and long-term credit on a vast scale, the progressive sophistication of its techniques . . . represents a financial mechanism without precedent in other countries.[10]

However, the predominant role of monetary instruments for stabilization, together with the increasing dependence of enterprise investment on bank loans in more recent years has meant that restrictive policies tend to have a direct and severe impact on productive investment even when longer-term (or even short-term) growth and employment objectives would rather dictate prior restraint of consumption. Yet in conditions of spontaneous slackening of final demand for exports or consumption, monetary expansion, while *permitting* more investment, may not *induce* it. In more general terms, monetary measures appropriate to internal demand conditions may be inappropriate to the pattern of capital flows across the exchanges and/or to the Government's internal borrowing requirements.

Moreover, throughout the post-war period the objectives of economic policy have not been confined to short-term demand management in the interests of balance-of-payments equilibrium, or price stability, or avoidance of cyclical employment fluctuations. Two elements that have always been present were first the need to keep up a strong growth of over-all demand and of investment in productive capacity so as to overcome as soon as possible the long-term unemployment (or economic development) problem and, secondly, the complication of structural imbalances calling for discriminating measures taking account of regional and sectoral disequilibria and the co-existence of full employment in some sectors or regions with unemployment and under-employment in others.

The ideal of 'as many policy measures as there are policy objectives' remains unrealized in more countries than Italy. But the overwhelming reliance on monetary measures in Italy appears notably inadequate to the complicated nature of economic problems and objectives.

The financial system and monetary instruments

An excellent study on *Monetary Policy in Italy* was published by the O.E.C.D. in 1973. It contains a detailed analysis of institutions, instruments, and techniques, as well as of the impact of monetary measures on financial variables and on private expenditures, which it would serve no purpose to duplicate here. This brief survey will limit itself to a summary of some of the main findings, supplemented by information from other sources, particularly on developments since 1971 (not covered by the O.E.C.D. study) and on some controversial questions raised by Italian authors about the role monetary policy may have played in slowing down investment, even in periods when the official policy stance was expansionary. More specifically, some attention is given to the problems for monetary policy arising from the need to defend bond prices in the face of an enormous increase in issues, especially of Treasury bonds, and to the efforts made by the monetary authorities to prevent the balance-of-payments constraint from interfering unduly with the pursuit of policies to stimulate productive activity.

The pattern of financial flows in Italy is characterized by the following main features: a large financial deficit of the enterprise sector, largely dependent for its external financing on borrowing from banks and special credit institutions while security issues by private enterprises play a very minor role; substantial and growing Treasury deficits financed by short-term credit from the Bank of Italy and by issues of Government bonds, while the local authorities rely on banks, special credit institutions, and central budget funds to finance their deficits; the predominantly liquid forms in which households hold their savings (shown on page 59).

The Italian monetary system which channels these financial flows is comparatively simple. It consists of the Central Bank, commercial and savings banks, the special credit institutions, and the Central Post Office Fund. Insurance companies play a negligible role as lenders and no specialized financial institutions for special categories of credit, such as instalment credit, exist. The scope for selectivity between consumer and investment credit is thus very limited.

Banks supply on average close to one-half of the funds borrowed by the non-financial sector and the special credit institutions account for some 20 per cent. The latter grant medium- and long-term loans, largely at subsidized interest rates, to the household and enterprise sector and raise their funds mainly through long-term bond issues at home and abroad, while part of the interest subsidy is contributed by the budget. The Central Post Office Fund supplies some 6 per cent of total lending, mainly to local authorities.

Another characteristic feature of the Italian financial system is the exceptionally large size of bond issues. These are dominated by the Government, the special credit institutions and the state-holding companies, while private issues play a very minor role. The banking system takes up, on average, between 50 and 60 per cent of the issues, and 'households' almost all the remainder. The stabilization of bond prices between 1966 and 1969 (see below) sustained demand for bonds by the public, and when pegging was abandoned the share of households in the absorption of bonds declined.

New issues of shares are relatively large compared with other O.E.C.D. countries; but investment in shares by households and financial institutions continues to be low and a major part of share issues is absorbed by other companies and by the 'rest of the world'.

Finally the Italian financial system is characterized by a virtual absence of an active money market such as operates in some other countries.

The financial pattern and institutions in Italy permit far-reaching control over credit flows by the monetary authorities. All banks are subject to minimum reserve requirements, and security issues beyond a specified amount—whether by special credit institutions, private or public enterprises, or local authorities—are subject to prior approval.

The formal instruments used for regulating the supply and cost of credit are: changes in availability and cost of Central Bank credit to commercial banks; variations in minimum reserve requirements; debt management operations; and changes in directives concerning the commercial banks' net foreign position. Among the available instruments, control of fund-raising, subsidization of lending by special credit institutions, control over new issues, and sales and purchases of government securities have been used rather more for structural purposes—to channel finance to specific sectoral or regional objectives or to enlarge and improve the bond market—than for general stabilization. For short-run influence the monetary authorities have relied mainly on changes in Central Bank credit and directives to banks on variations of their net foreign indebtedness.

Since the mid-sixties, the whole monetary base rather than, as previously, bank-reserves regulation has become the operational quantity variable of monetary policy. But the stabilization of interest rates on long-term bonds was an intermediate target from 1966 to 1969. The 'monetary base' is defined as liquid claims on the rest of the world, the Government, and the Central Bank held by the private sector, including the commercial banks and specialized financial institutions. While there may not be an absolutely precise and predictable connection between variations in this aggregate and the total money supply, or the availability of credit to the non-bank private sector, the monetary base is in fact regarded as a major policy variable. It is created through three channels: changes in the net impact of the foreign sector; Treasury deficits net of long-term bond sales; and the banking system. The Bank of Italy exercises a strong influence on all three channels. It can offset the net impact of the foreign sector on the monetary base (but also on official foreign exchange reserves) through changing directives to banks on their net foreign credit or debit positions. The growing Treasury deficits have become the most important source of expansion of the monetary base in recent years; and these can be partially offset through a reduction of Bank of Italy credit and through sales of government bonds, though the Central Bank has felt constrained at times to purchase substantial amounts of long-term government bonds so as to support prices and sustain public demand for them in the longer term. The Bank of Italy has a direct and discretionary control over the commercial banking system, which has been operated rather through variations in the volume of bank credit than through variations in its cost except when manipulation of interest rates was itself a policy aim.*

But while the monetary authorities have a substantial degree of control over monetary variables, they have had to become increasingly concerned with external considerations as the international interdependence of financial centres grew. In addition, the need to finance budget deficits of recent dimensions has constrained domestic monetary policy. The enormous size of bond issues has therefore progressively turned monetary policy into an instrument for equilibrating the bond market. The difficulties for the monetary authorities which arose, and might continue to arise, from conflicting internal and external objectives and contradictory domestic claims are illustrated in a brief description of various policy phases.

Policy phases

The first test of monetary policy as a counter-cyclical instrument, in the inflation and recession of 1963–5, has been discussed earlier and the rapid response to monetary restraint followed by a delayed and weak reaction to a reflationary course has already been described.

The subsequent phase which lasted from mid-1966 to mid-1969 has been termed an 'accommodating phase' in the O.E.C.D. study. The monetary authorities decided to stabilize long-term bond rates—both private and public—in the face of a rapid rise in the supply of bonds, due mainly to Treasury borrowing requirements. This implied a willingness to see large changes in the monetary base, yet at the same time annual money-supply targets began to be officially established. In the event, government and other bond yields hardly changed during the period while the monetary base

* For a more technical analysis of the impact of changes in the monetary base on monetary aggregates, interest rates, and capital flows, see the O.E.C.D. study, *Monetary Policy in Italy*, Paris, 1973.

increased by very similar amounts from year to year (see Tables 11 and 12).

Criticism of the Bank of Italy's policy has focused on the double question of why productive investment responded so slowly and weakly to monetary stimulation and why it did not rise faster than it did during the period of 'accommodation'.[11] It must be recalled that—although productive investment did, in fact, increase rapidly from 1966 to 1968—first, it took a long time to make up for the ground lost during the recession and, secondly, the absorption of idle labour resources would have required still higher rates of expansion. Thus it was thought by some that monetary policy had, in reality, had a restrictive impact on investment although the pegged interest rate was considered to be moderately expansionary by the monetary authorities and the balance-of-payments constraint, they considered, prevented their setting a lower rate. It was argued that when general government deficits began to assume considerable proportions the monetary authorities were operating under two internal constraints: to restrict the money supply to the limit beyond which inflation might threaten and to restrict bond issues to a level which would not produce a fall in bond prices. With an over-cautious evaluation of the physical margins for expansion, limits were set for these two magnitudes which resulted in a conflict between the financing needs of the private and public sectors. In the view of Professor Sylos-Labini and others, the monetary authorities, by underestimating the available non-inflationary growth potential, set the additional money creation at too low a level. Thus, while inflation was prevented, an unnecessary brake was placed on private investment.

At the same time, however, public investment expenditure did not materialize at the anticipated level. This was not—as has often been argued—the consequence of an excessive planned increase in *current* public expenditure. Because of an exaggerated preoccupation with inflation, the authorities have sometimes sought to check both capital and current expenditure. When it was considered necessary to step up public expenditure as a whole, it was easier and quicker to accelerate current expenditure; and it was thus the rigidity of public investment—the failure rapidly to expand outlays—which caused, in a sense, the rapid increases of current spending. The result has been a shift in the composition of public expenditure, at the expense of public investment, which reduced the multiplier effect of the budget deficit. In addition, a smaller investment component of total public expenditure limited the expansion of social infrastructures and contributed to mounting social pressures.

The accusation that the Bank of Italy's policies have not been aggressive enough to bring about a sufficiently rapid expansion does assume, however, that monetary policy alone could have stimulated demand sufficiently to raise actual output to the supply potential. It further assumes that demand alone constituted an obstacle to more rapid growth. But it must be borne in mind that supply factors were also responsible for insufficient expansion. These consisted in, among others, the special structural conditions of the labour market (analysed in Part Two), the weakening of the previous dynamism of Italian enterprise, and the political uncertainties and social tensions already referred to. All these factors were independent of the supply or cost of finance.

In the early part of 1969 and until the summer of 1970 monetary policy again became restrictive, at first to check the deterioration of the balance of payments and subsequently also for domestic reasons. For the former purpose, banks were instructed to reduce their net foreign assets; measures were taken to check capital flight in the form of the export of lira banknotes, and the pre-payment period for imports and delays for repatriating export receipts were shortened.

The pegging of long-term government bond rates was abandoned, since the gap between Italian and foreign interest rates had increasingly widened; but the Bank of Italy nevertheless supported government security prices through massive purchases and the monetary authorities proceeded to ration new issues. The total outcome of these measures, however, was that interest rates began to rise, and security prices to fall, somewhat in 1969 and very sharply in 1970.

The discount rate was raised in two steps, in the summer of 1969 and in March of 1970. The balance-of-payments deficit reduced the monetary base but the financing by the Bank of Italy of the Treasury's deficit more than offset the decline and the total monetary base increased in 1969 by the same amount as in 1968. Thus, whereas the increase of the monetary base had halved in the first restrictive phase of 1963 compared so the previous year but interest rates had risen very little, this time 'restriction' produced higher interest rates though continuing expansion of the monetary base; and the rates of price inflation and growth of money national income were not higher in the second period than in the first.

The slow-down in the rate of expansion of real demand and output, particularly of investment, in 1970 became more pronounced in 1971, and stimulating measures were taken and progressively reinforced. At first monetary conditions eased, as the demand for credit slackened and the increase in the monetary base speeded up in the fourth quarter of 1970. An expansionary impetus was provided by the balance of payments and the financing of the budget deficit. In addition, the Bank of Italy reduced the discount rate in March 1970 and in April and October 1971 and lowered the rate on advances in January and October 1971. But the substantial increase in financial flows in 1971 both to the public and the private sector did not find a counterpart in an increase in private investment. The larger volume of financing was used in part to cover the losses incurred by the industrial sector and, for the rest, to reconstitute margins of liquidity.

In 1972 all monetary aggregates continued to show a strong upward tendency and interest rates to decline. But a progressive worsening of the balance of payments slowed down the growth of the monetary base in the second half of the year while the demand for credit accelerated with the incipient upturn of economic activity and investment.

Monetary policy had to contend with increasing difficulties in reconciling support for vulnerable expansion with financing the enormous increase in public indebtedness and limiting the rapid rise of capital outflows. One first step in the effort to free monetary policy from the balance-of-payments constraint was to counteract the restrictive impact on liquidity arising from the currency crisis of June 1972 by once again authorizing banks to increase their foreign indebtedness; and this was followed by the major decision in 1973 to institute a double lira market and to let the lira fluctuate.

On the domestic front an increasing constraint was placed on policy decisions through the rapidly growing financial needs of the public administration. Total securities in circulation had risen from 13,000 billion lire at the end of 1965 to 41,000 billion at the end of 1972. Of these, Treasury issues had expanded from 4,000 to 16,000 billion lire, and the Bank of Italy has increasingly felt compelled to act in defence of security prices.

Should it become necessary to proceed to a containment of the global volume of credit, this would be concentrated on the productive sector because of the rigidity of demand of the public sector. There would be once again a loud outcry; the responsibility would be attributed to the monetary authorities while in fact it lies with the diffused incapacity to administer with modern concepts, a capacity for innovation, and a clarity of views. This sequel of events will become inevitable if proposals for additional government expenditure are not rejected.

While the efficiency of the Central Bank has been generally recognized,

we find it necessary to express a warning that the increase in efficiency was accompanied by a limitation of the possibility to manifest it through concrete action set by the counter-acting behaviour of the public authorities. The conciliation of objectives must precede and not follow the actions of monetary policy.[12]

Concluding remarks

Conclusions on the impact of monetary policy on real private demand and expenditure cannot be quantified on the basis of available information. The impact on investment was apparently strong in both phases of restraint (1963–4 and

1969–70) but, as has already been pointed out, this could hardly be ascribed entirely or perhaps even predominantly to credit restrictions. Other factors such as labour conflicts, low profits, poor business expectations and the general economic and political climate have also played a role. Further, demand restraint within feasible limits could not be expected to achieve the goal of price stability in periods of rising costs and, in so far as it slowed down productive investment, it also checked productivity increases and had a 'perverse' effect on unit labour costs and prices.

It is evident that 'other factors' were responsible for the slow response of investment demand to monetary stimulation, to which must be added the special conditions affecting investment in housing in recent years. The fact that investment did not rise faster than it did during the phase of accommodation, and interest rate pegging, may have been partly due to conflicting claims between the financing of private and public expenditure and an over-cautious evaluation by the monetary authorities of the physical margin for expansion.

As to the long-term aim of filling the gap between actual and potential output with the help of monetary instruments, the O.E.C.D. report concludes that 'the slack in the Italian economy could not have been reduced substantially by monetary expansion in the range of the policy options which may be considered feasible.'

Monetary policy did, however, have a more decisive impact on the capital account of the balance of payments, although the wish to stabilize interest rates to facilitate the financing of the budget deficit, at a time when interest rates were rising elsewhere, produced a conflict between external and internal objectives. More direct action on the external account became necessary, through measures to prevent the export of banknotes and through provisions regulating banks' and public corporations' net foreign indebtedness, and these proved successful on some occasions, particularly in 1969–70.

Italian experience appears to be a good illustration of the general proposition that, in an open economy with fixed exchange rates, monetary policy is more effective in achieving the external aims of a balance on non-monetary transactions than in influencing domestic policy objectives.[13]

However, when speculative factors, rather than interest rate differentials, became predominant in provoking huge capital outflows after the international currency crisis of June 1972, the Italian monetary authorities felt compelled to choose the abandonment of the fixed lira parity as a way out. (See the next section for more recent measures to stem capital outflows.)

CHAPTER 4

THE BALANCE OF PAYMENTS AND THE LIRA

FROM the latter part of the 1950s onwards, the Italian balance of payments was characterized by surpluses on current account. The sole exceptions were 1963 and those months of 1973 for which data are so far available. The surplus rose more than threefold from 1964 to 1965, remained large through most of the following years, declined sharply in 1970, doubled again in 1971, and about maintained the previous year's level in 1972 (see Table 6). The current surpluses were virtually matched by an outflow of capital in all years from 1962 onwards, except for 1964; and the over-all balance on non-monetary transactions was in deficit in 1963 and again in 1969, 1972, and 1973.

For a labour-surplus country still lagging behind other industrial countries in the level of its development, the structure of the Italian balance of payments must be considered abnormal. One would have expected an external payments pattern showing a current deficit financed by an inflow of long-term capital. But in fact a sizeable share of Italy's gross savings was exported instead of being used to finance domestic capital formation (see Fig. 4); and while the share of exports of goods and services in GNP has risen from 14·5 per cent in 1961–2 to 26·2 per cent in 1971–2, the corresponding domestic investment ratios declined from 22·6 to 17·4 per cent.

In recent years the balance of payments has become more vulnerable for a number of reasons: (1) The elasticity of imports with respect to the growth of domestic demand has increased. (2) The elasticity of exports in relation to world demand has a tendency to stagnate: while the share of Italian exports of manufactures in the total of such exports from industrial countries had risen strongly for many years, reaching a peak of 7·3 per cent in 1968, it has since remained virtually stationary. (3) The growing dissociation between the sources of private-sector savings and decision-centres for investment, due to a shift from enterprise to household savings, led to substantial transfers of savings to foreign financial centres. (4) Alternative financial investment outlets, in particular the Eurodollar market, offered more attractive conditions as to yield and fiscal treatment, advantages of anonymity, greater flexibility and diversification. (5) The ratio of official reserves to the annual volume of foreign transactions declined from 21 per cent in 1962 to 10 per cent in 1972. If gold reserves at the end of 1972 are excluded (to take account of the present status of gold in international settlements) this ratio is reduced to 5 per cent.

Moreover, there has been a shift among the various factors responsible for capital outflows. It has been estimated that autonomous capital exports due to interest rate differentials have lost in relative importance, their share in the total declining from 30 per cent in 1969 to 4 per cent in 1972. Capital exports caused by profit rate differences and by 'other causes' of a speculative nature increased enormously from preceding years both in 1969 and in 1972, accounting for 40 and 47 per cent respectively of the total, while the capital outflow due to commercial leads and lags (also largely speculative) rose to an all-time high in 1972 and was responsible for 30 per cent of total capital exports.[1]

The increasingly speculative nature of capital exports implies that the balance of payments has become less amenable to traditional measures of monetary restraint, though monetary stimulation of domestic demand may still tend to accentuate capital outflows.

> A situation in which the supply of money exceeds demand can result not only in an increased demand for domestic real or financial assets but also in a demand for foreign currency and securities when that situation is accompanied by an increase in the differential between domestic and foreign interest and profit rates and by speculative phenomena. . . . To provide the economy with liquidity and only end up aggravating the balance-of-payments deficit is like offering wine to a drunkard.[2]

The factors most recently affecting trade and capital flows have rendered the reconciliation of domestic and external policy goals more difficult than in the past. The monetary authorities have become increasingly—and perhaps excessively—concerned with the reconstitution of international reserves to a level they consider adequate for freeing future growth and employment objectives from balance-of-payments constraints. In the view of the Governor of the Bank of Italy, a wider margin for manoeuvre became essential as speculative pressures became more violent and more frequent.

A chronology of events

In recent years the Italian balance of payments has repeatedly been subject to considerable strains requiring corrective measures by the monetary authorities; and these culminated early in 1973 in the institution of a double lira exchange market and the decision to let the lira exchange rate fluctuate.

In 1969 the over-all balance on non-monetary transactions closed with a sizeable deficit after five years of balance-of-payments surpluses. The trade surplus of the previous year was almost halved as disruptions of production caused by the autumn strikes slowed down exports and accelerated the rise of imports; and at the same time net capital outflows more than doubled. Interest rate differentials played a substantial role in causing capital exports; but loss of confidence in the currency due to social unrest and political uncertainty, as well as expectations of a revaluation of the German Mark, predominated. Illegal exports of banknotes, almost entirely directed to Switzerland, accounted for more than 60 per cent of the total net capital outflow. Official reserves declined relatively little, however, and a more important part of the deficit was financed by a reduction on the net foreign exchange assets of commercial banks.

A large swing from an over-all deficit of $1,391 million to a surplus of $356 million occurred in 1970. Supply difficulties and a temporary revival of domestic demand turned the trade balance into deficit and the net surplus on invisibles declined sharply. But these adverse changes were more than offset by a marked improvement of the capital account, thanks largely to a series of policy measures. Measures taken to reverse interest rate differentials in favour of Italy have been described, and borrowing abroad by state-holding companies and special credit institutions increased substantially. In February 1970 the Bank of Italy withdrew its authorization to Italian banks to receive lira banknotes sent back to Italy by foreign banks and presentation to the Central Bank for conversion became compulsory. This involved a higher cost for operators, deriving from the longer delay until repatriated banknotes could be credited and from a higher discount and, with the reversal of interest rate differentials, checked the outflow of capital in this form (from $2,256 million in 1969 to $951 million in 1970). At the same time the permitted pre-payment period for imports and delay for the repatriation of export proceeds were curtailed.

In 1971 the balance of payments was affected by the domestic recession and by buoyant world trade. The balance of trade turned into surplus again, and the total surplus on current account doubled and, although the capital outflow accelerated very sharply, the over-all surplus on non-monetary transactions more than doubled.

Capital movements showed divergent tendencies in the course of the year. In the early part of 1971 there was a substantial net inflow of long-term funds, accounted for mainly by massive borrowing by the state-holding companies. The large net outflow in the latter part of the year was due to accelerated repayments of public debts contracted in the two preceding years, rendered possible by the improved balance-of-payments position.

Speculative factors linked to the dollar crisis affected the Italian currency only marginally, partly because of a series of precautionary measures taken by the monetary authorities, partly because expectations of a lira revaluation were less than for some other currencies and partly also because in the prevailing recessionary conditions the attraction for speculative funds was less in Italy than elsewhere. The substantial increase in official reserves in 1971 amounted to 25 per cent in terms of dollars but—as a consequence of the currency realignments of December 1971—to 19 per cent in lira.

From June 1972 onwards, the Italian balance of payments was repeatedly subject to acute pressures arising from international currency crises and domestic speculative attacks on the currency. In the five preceding months Italy's external accounts had developed rather favourably, a sizeable surplus on current account permitting the continuation of the policy of advance reimbursement of outstanding foreign loans. But in June the deterioration of the British balance of payments and the announcement that the British Government's domestic objectives would be given priority over balance-of-payments considerations caused expectations of a devaluation of sterling and large international capital movements. After a brief closure of exchange markets, the British Government decided to let sterling fluctuate and, although the Italian balance-of-payments position was fairly solid at the time, international events and the inflationary situation at home created expectations that the lira would follow the sterling devaluation. Speculative attacks compelled the Bank of Italy to disburse vast amounts of foreign currencies in defence of the lira exchange rate.

A series of measures were once again taken to check capital flight. In June the Bank of Italy announced that it would suspend the crediting of Italian banknotes posted from abroad; the policy of borrowing abroad by banks and special credit institutions was resumed and authorization to take net creditor positions discontinued; and a loan of half a billion dollars was obtained from U.S. banks.

Action in defence of Italy's international reserves was supplemented by a policy to influence their composition. Under the Basle agreement of April 1972, the Common Market countries undertook to limit fluctuations of their currencies to 2·25 per cent of their par values (the 'snake in the tunnel'). Any intervention within the prescribed limits had to be effected in Community currencies, settlement in dollars being permitted only when the exchange rate had reached the established limits. If a member was short of the necessary Community currencies, it could call on reciprocal credit lines established between central banks. The repayment of debts thus incurred was to take place in currencies in the same proportion as the composition of official reserves of the debtor country. Italy succeeded in obtaining a partial derogation of these rules. From the end of June until the end of 1972, the lira exchange rate could be defended through exclusive intervention in dollars, which constituted by far the major part of Italy's convertible currency reserves, instead of in Community currencies. A settlement of debts through international means of payment in proportion to the composition of reserves would, moreover, have involved large settlements in gold, which was a still larger component of Italian international reserves. Since the market price of gold was much higher than its official price, and since the role of gold in the international monetary system had not yet been defined, it would have been practically impossible to reconstitute gold reserves in the event of a reversal of Italy's foreign accounts.

After the June–July international currency crisis, the lira continued to be subject to speculative pressures from within. These took the form of commercial leads and lags and of large capital exports for portfolio investment, interest rate differentials playing only a minor causal role. There was also a deficit on current account, despite a marked expansion of exports, as the volume of imports of raw and semi-processed materials rose with the recovery of domestic production, and import prices also increased. Moreover, the suspension of the crediting of repatriated banknotes and the resulting decline in the banknote exchange rate reduced income from tourism and from emigrants' remittances.

The outcome for the year 1972 as a whole was a current account surplus rather less than the previous year's and a doubled rate of outflow of capital. The over-all balance turned into a deficit almost as large as that of 1969; official reserves declined sharply, the reduction being concentrated on dollars, and the net foreign indebtedness of commercial banks increased very substantially.

At the beginning of 1973 another devaluation scare produced renewed speculative capital outflows which, together with a continuing current deficit, caused enormous losses of official reserves. The Italian monetary authorities felt compelled to introduce a double exchange market for the commercial and financial lira in January and to float the currency in February. The latter decision was severely criticized both abroad and in Italy. It was argued by some that the Italian monetary authorities had deliberately provoked a disguised devaluation and that the steps taken involved a loosening of Italy's ties with the European Economic Community. The official justifications were that the mere fact of the defence measures taken was proof that there had been no intention to let the exchange rate deteriorate; that adherence to the margins of fluctuation stipulated by the Basle agreement would have resulted in further major losses of reserves, and hence the necessity to devalue at some later stage *without* sufficient reserves to contain the extent of the devaluation; that monetary restraint would stifle the renewed expansion and that it could have but little effect on capital movements caused largely by speculative factors and only to a very limited extent by interest rate differentials; finally, that a certain flexibility of exchange rates was necessary to reconcile divergences in conjunctural developments and economic policies in Common Market countries, in the absence of their effective co-ordination, and that the European Fund for Monetary Co-operation, soon to be set up, would not dispose of sufficient means to ensure that losses of reserves would not lead to a devaluation.

Subsequently, criticisms were voiced against the decision to adopt a fluctuating rate rather than a once-over devaluation. It was argued that there had in fact been no fluctuation, but rather a step-by-step devaluation which had tended to encourage speculation and capital flight rather than to prevent it. Moreover, though a *de facto* devaluation might be needed to maintain the competitive position of Italian exports while reconstituting profit margins as a stimulus to industrial investment, *progressive* devaluation encouraged a feeling that domestic cost and price inflation could safely continue unchecked. Gradual devaluation had thus fed both speculation and inflation.[3]

Other experts who had previously criticized the excessive concern of the monetary authorities with the balance-of-payments position, who had opposed devaluation in the autumn of 1972, and who were also in political opposition to the government in power at the time, held the view that this time the exceptionally heavy losses of reserves and the continuing pressure on the lira did not leave another way out.

After the decision to float the lira the exchange rate depreciated fast. Soon after floating, the average rate of devaluation reached 8 per cent; by early June it was 12 per cent; by mid-June the news that the Bank of Italy had asked the Federal Reserve Bank to sell 13 billion lira in exchange for foreign currencies to meet debt repayments which the Bank of Italy could not cover from its own foreign currency reserves set off another speculative wave and after the so-called 'black Thursday' of 14 June, the average devaluation rate increased sharply to 21·75 per cent. Subsequently there was a gradual strengthening and by the end of August this rate was between 10 and 11 per cent below the 'pre-float' parity. But while the lira had appreciated somewhat in relation to the dollar, its devaluation *vis-à-vis* the strong European currencies and the yen remained rather substantial.

The partial recovery of the lira was perhaps due in part to a revival of confidence, following the announcement of an emergency programme by the Centro-Sinistra Government to deal with price inflation, the enormous budget deficit and other problems; and the strengthening of the currency itself contributed to a reversal of leads and lags, to raising foreign currency receipts from tourism and to speculative capital inflows. It was more specifically due to certain measures decided upon in July: selective credit restrictions (described in the concluding chapter together with the other parts of the package deal) and a tightening of controls over capital exports. The latter imposed an obligation, on Italian residents wishing to invest abroad, to deposit into a frozen and non-interest-bearing account, with the bank making the investment on their behalf, lire equal to 50 per cent (or for some types of investment 25 per cent) of the amount to be placed abroad. In addition, advance payments for imports of goods and services can only be made with foreign currencies obtained from Italian banks and delayed payments for imports of goods and services are altogether prohibited. The former provision is to prevent importers obtaining currency from other than official sources; the latter aims to prevent importers choosing the most propitious moment for settling their debts. Other controls over foreign exchange transactions have also been tightened.

The basic questions of when to terminate the double exchange market and the fluctuation of the lira, what rate of official devaluation to decide upon, and under what conditions to submit again to the rules of monetary co-operation within the European Economic Community figure as major issues on the policy programme of the Government. The decisions depend both on developments on the international monetary scene and on the success or failure in checking capital outflows and in solving problems of domestic balance.

APPENDIX TO PART ONE

TABLES AND FIGURES

Table 1

Gross national product in selected countries,
1954–1963 and 1963–1972
annual percentage increases at constant prices

	1954–63	1963–72[1]
Austria	6·0	5·0
Belgium	3·5	4·6
France	5·3	5·7
West Germany	6·6	4·5
Italy	5·6	4·7
Netherlands	4·5	5·3
Sweden	4·1	3·7
United Kingdom	2·8	2·8
O.E.C.D. Europe	3·9	4·6
United States	3·1	3·6

1. Except for Italy, the figures for 1972 are estimates.

Sources: Italy: ISTAT, *Annuario di contabilità nazionale* (1971); Ministero del Bilancio e della Programmazione Economica, *Relazione Generale* (1972). Other countries: O.E.C.D., *National Accounts of O.E.C.D. Countries.*

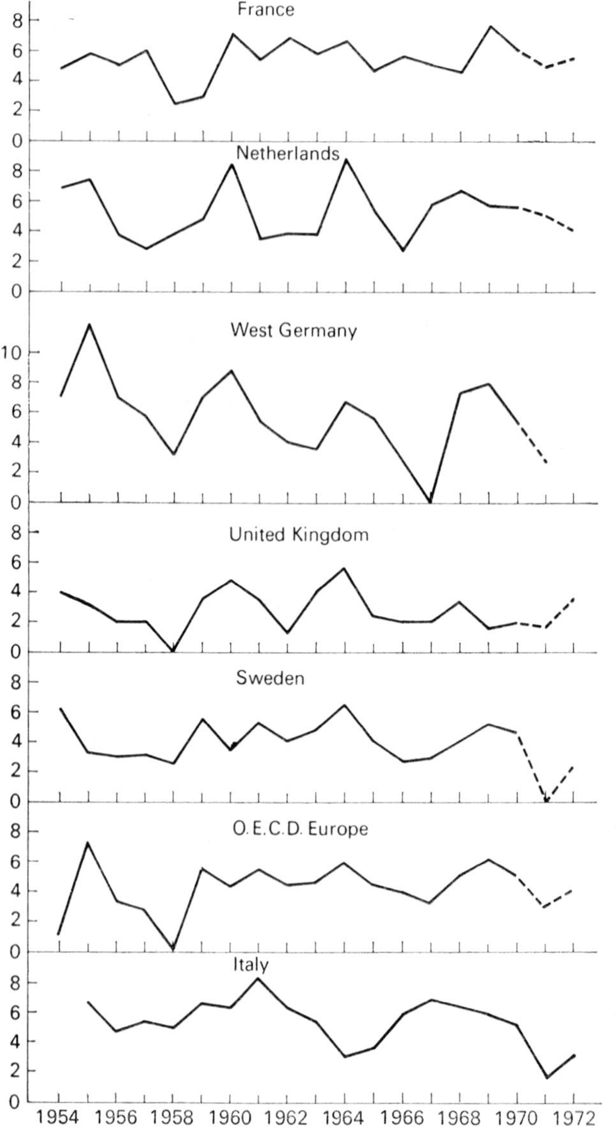

FIG. 1 *Gross national product in selected countries, 1953–1972. Percentage changes from previous years at constant prices*

Note: Except for Italy, the figures for 1972 are estimates.

Sources: Italy: ISTAT, *Annuario di contabilità nazionale* (1971); Ministero del Bilancio e della Programmazione Economica, *Relazione Generale* (1972).

Other countries: O.E.C.D., *National Accounts of O.E.C.D. Countries.*

TABLE 2

Supply and use of resources 1952–1972, annual percentage increases at constant prices

	1952–62 average	'62	'63	'64	'65	'66	'67	'68	'69	'70	'71	'72
RESOURCES												
GNP at market prices	5·9	6·3	5·4	2·9	3·6	5·9	6·8	6·4	5·9	5·1	1·6	3·2
Imports of goods and services	13·5	16·4	22·4	−5·1	1·9	13·7	13·1	7·5	20·6	17·2	1·7	13·2
Total	6·2	7·5	7·6	1·7	3·4	7·0	7·7	6·6	8·2	7·2	1·6	5·1
UTILIZATION												
Private consumption	5·0	6·5	8·9	3·0	2·7	6·8	7·1	4·9	6·3	8·0	2·8	3·8
Public consumption	3·8	5·4	4·6	3·6	4·0	3·2	4·3	4·1	3·3	3·2	5·2	4·2
Gross fixed capital formation	10·2	10·1	8·1	−6·4	−8·6	4·0	11·8	9·7	8·0	3·6	−3·5	−0·2
of which:												
Residential construction	13·0	15·4	12·1	6·9	−6·2	−1·3	5·6	11·9	15·1	−6·1	−12·0	1·7
Other construction	8·8	12·6	0·4	−3·0	−2·1	2·6	10·4	6·5	3·1	2·5	2·3	−2·5
Machinery and plant	9·1	8·3	7·4	−18·7	−19·5	14·7	15·6	9·8	7·1	15·5	1·6	−0·5
Transport equipment	10·4	9·1	22·3	−11·7	−5·1	0·3	24·6	11·2	3·2	6·7	0·1	1·4
Exports of goods and services	13·7	12·3	6·9	11·6	20·1	13·2	6·7	15·4	13·8	6·0	6·0	11·2

Sources: ISTAT, *Annuario di contabilità nazionale* (1971); Ministero del Bilancio e della Programmazione Economica, *Relazione Generale* (1971 and 1972).

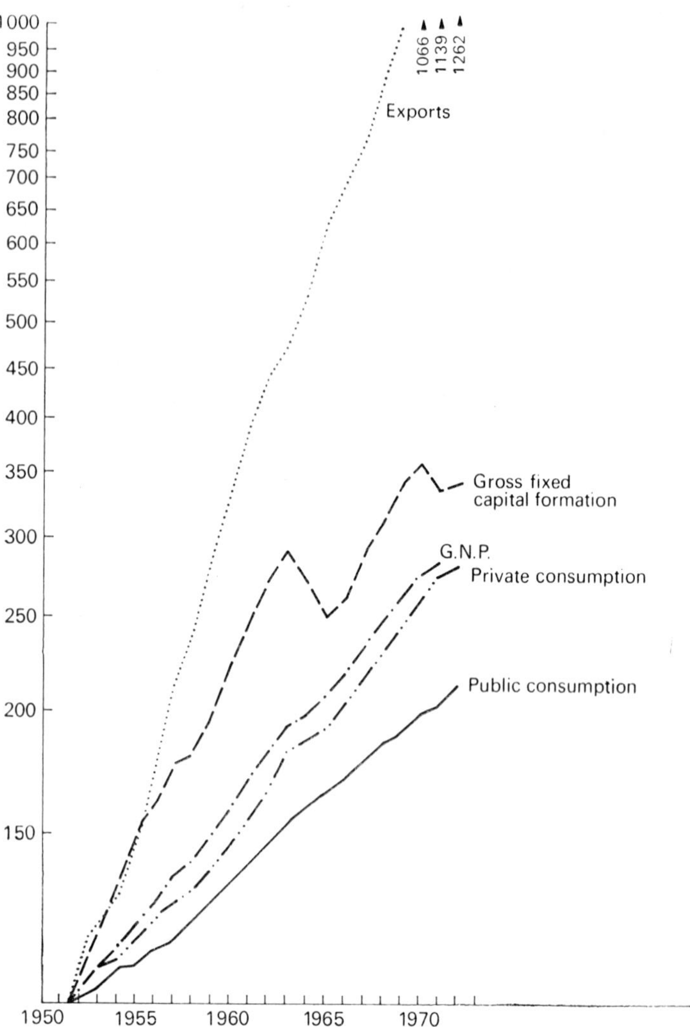

FIG. 2 *Growth of GNP and main sectors of demand, 1950–1972. At 1963 prices, average 1951–2 = 100*
Source: ISTAT, *Annuario di contabilità nazionale* (1971).

TABLE 3

Price developments 1952–1972, annual percentage increases

	1952	'53	'54	'55	'56	'57	'58	'59	'60	'61	'62	'63	'64	'65	'66	'67	'68	'69	'70	'71	'72
Implied price deflator of GNP	3·2	2·8	2·8	3·4	3·9	2·0	2·3	−0·2	2·0	2·7	5·7	8·7	6·3	3·9	2·2	3·0	1·5	4·1	6·3	6·6	5·9
Wholesale prices of non-agricultural goods	..	..	−1·3	0·5	0·5	2·1	−2·9	−1·9	0·8	−0·3	1·5	4·9	4·5	0·9	1·3	0·0	0·0	3·6	8·1	3·4	3·4
Consumer prices	..	..	2·9	2·3	3·4	1·3	2·9	−0·6	2·4	2·1	4·6	7·6	5·9	4·5	2·3	3·7	1·3	2·7	5·0	4·8	5·7
Imports, *unit values*	−1·8	−7·8	−4·1	1·4	3·2	5·3	−12·1	−7·0	−1·3	−2·3	0·2	1·7	0·6	0·3	1·2	1·0	0·5	1·4	3·8	7·8	1·5
Exports, *unit values*	−5·2	−0·9	−2·9	−3·0	−2·4	3·4	−4·7	−8·0	4·0	−3·4	0·9	1·2	1·4	0·3	−1·1	0·9	−0·5	3·7	5·2	6·1	1·2

Sources: ISTAT; for 1972, Bank of Italy, *Relazione Annuale*.

TABLE 4

Output, employment, productivity, wages, unit labour costs, and profits in manufacturing, 1954–1972 annual percentage increases

	average 1954–61	'61	'62	'63	'64	'65	'66	'67	'68	'69	'70	'71	'72
Output[1]	8·0	10·3	10·7	6·5	1·3	5·2	9·2	9·9	9·3	6·5	8·0	−0·1	4·2
Employment	2·1	4·8	2·5	2·0	−0·2	−2·6	0·6	3·6	1·0	1·8	3·2	0·2	−0·5
Hours worked	2·1	3·8	−0·3	2·3	−4·4	−5·4	3·6	4·1	0·7	−1·9	3·1	−3·4	−2·4
Output per man	6·0	5·2	8·0	4·4	1·5	8·0	8·5	6·1	8·3	4·5	4·6	−0·3	4·7
Output per man-hour	5·7	6·3	11·1	4·1	6·4	10·8	5·4	5·6	8·6	8·5	4·7	3·4	6·7
Wage rates[2]	4·5	4·4	10·7	14·7	14·0	8·5	3·9	5·5	3·6	7·5	21·6	13·5	10·4
Hourly earnings	4·9	7·0	15·3	16·8	11·1	7·4	3·9	6·2	4·5	9·9	23·9	16·0	10·5
Unit labour cost	−0·3	1·2	5·3	14·5	5·2	−3·4	−2·0	0·4	−0·1	4·4	13·7	12·8	6·1
Unit profits[3]	−1·0	2·1	−8·7	−9·1	4·0	13·8	10·9	−8·7	5·4	3·9	−7·9	−18·4	8·0
Gross profit ratio[4]	45·1	41·8	38·6	34·8	34·7	37·2	39·0	36·5	36·6	36·5	33·1	27·9	40·3
Non-agricultural wholesale prices	−0·2	−0·2	1·4	4·9	4·4	0·9	1·3	0·0	0·0	3·6	8·1	3·4	3·4

1. Value added in manufacturing.
2. The base of the index was changed in 1966.
3. Gross profits per unit of output.
4. Value added minus compensation of employees as a ratio of value added—actual ratios, *not* annual percentage increases.

Sources: ISTAT, and data supplied by the Bank of Italy.

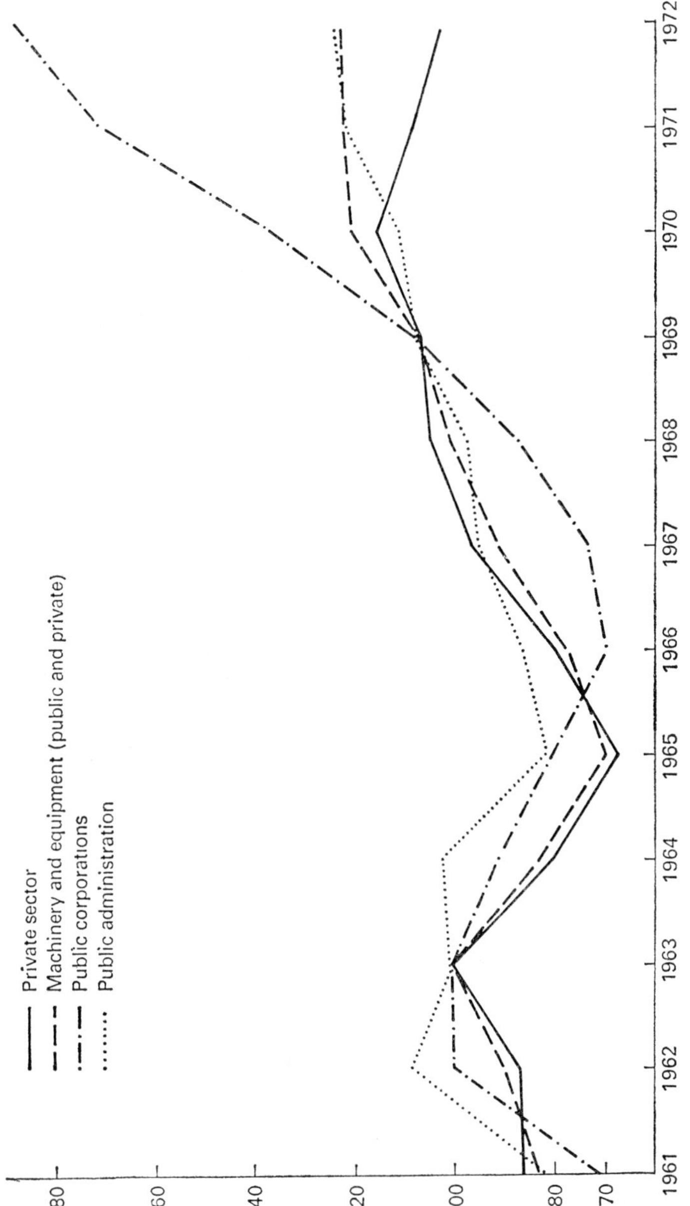

FIG. 3 *Private and public productive investment, 1961–1972*
Indices (1963 = 100) at constant prices
Sources: O.E.C.D., *Economic Surveys, Italy* (1972); for 1972, Bank of Italy.

Table 5

Distribution of national income 1961–1972, percentage shares

	1961	'62	'63	'64	'65	'66	'67	'68	'69	'70	'71	'72
Share of households and independent traders	95·1	95·8	96·7	96·8	95·6	95·2	95·5	95·0	95·0	96·4	97·6	97·0
Compensation of employees	51·9	53·6	56·8	58·0	57·1	56·3	56·5	56·6	56·4	59·0	62·4	62·9
Income of independent traders	33·8	33·2	31·5	30·5	30·2	30·2	30·0	28·9	29·1	27·8	26·0	25·3
Interest, rent, and dividends	9·4	9·0	8·4	8·3	8·3	8·7	9·0	9·5	9·5	9·6	9·2	8·8
Share of corporations	5·2	4·4	3·3	3·0	4·3	4·7	4·5	5·2	5·1	3·9	2·7	3·4
Direct taxes and transfers	2·3	2·5	2·3	2·1	2·2	2·1	2·3	2·2	2·1	1·9	1·9	2·0
Saving	2·9	1·9	1·0	0·9	2·1	2·6	2·2	3·0	3·0	2·0	0·8	1·4
Share of public administration	—0·3	—0·2	—	0·2	0·1	0·1	—	—0·2	—0·1	—0·3	—0·3	—0·4
Government income from property and entrepreneurship	2·3	2·3	2·3	2·4	2·5	2·6	2·6	2·6	2·7	2·7	3·0	3·1
Less: interest on the public debt	2·6	2·5	2·3	2·2	2·4	2·5	2·6	2·8	2·8	3·0	3·3	3·5
National income	100	100	100	100	100	100	100	100	100	100	100	100

Sources: ISTAT, *Annuano di contabilità nazionale* (1971); Ministero del Bilancio e della Programmazione Economica, *Relazione Generale* (1971 and 1972); for 1972, Bank of Italy estimates.

TABLE 6

The balance of payments 1960–1972, million dollars

	1960	'61	'62	'63	'64	'65	'66	'67	'68	'69	'70	'71	'72
Exports (FOB)	3570	4101	4590	4974	5863	7104	7929	8605	10098	11642	13117	14839	18441
Imports (FOB)	4216	4679	5505	6877	6508	6458	7595	8626	9050	11100	13498	14724	18439
Trade balance	−646	−578	−915	−1093	−645	646	334	−21	1048	542	−381	115	2
Services net	665	720	816	809	954	1221	1394	1257	1239	1386	956	1214	1023
Balance on goods and services	19	142	−99	−1094	309	1867	1728	1236	2287	1928	575	1329	1025
Transfers net	164	332	335	349	311	342	390	363	340	412	186	242	425
Current balance	283	474	236	−745	620	2209	2117	1599	2627	2340	761	1570	1450
Capital movements	73	187	−309	−485	110	−455	−1277	−1023	−1691	−3624	−237	−1150	−2313
Errors and omissions	81	−65	124	−21	44	−160	−145	−252	−309	−107	−168	−188	−422
Over-all balance on non-monetary transactions	437	551	51	−1252	774	1594	696	324	627	−1391	356	783	−1285

TABLE 6—*contd.*

Foreign reserves, end of period.	1960	'61	'62	'63	'64	'65	'66	'67	'68	'69	'70	'71	'72
Official reserves:													
Gold	2203	2225	2243	2343	2107	2404	2414	2400	2923	2956	2887	2884	2883
Convertible currencies	876	1194	1196	837	802	1462	1288	1419	958	898	2064	3063	2225
IMF position[1]	—	243	203	226	141	479	885	842	894	863	276	355	348
Special drawing rights	—	—	—	—	—	—	—	—	—	—	77	228	341
Other	1	87	162	11	706	219	92	577	133	−21	−33	−102	−98
Total official[2]	3080	3749	3804	3395	3756	4564	4679	5238	4878	4696	5271	6428	5699
Commercial banks: net foreign position	−135	−174	−605	−1254	−812	−178	230	35	723	36	17	−164	−603

1. The IMF position includes credits granted on a multilateral basis previously recorded under 'other' items.
2. Excluding medium- and long-term assets of the monetary authorities.
Source: Bank of Italy.

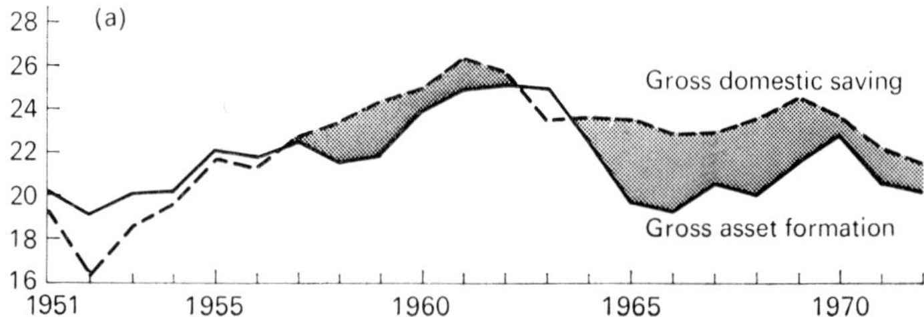

FIG. 4(*a*) *Saving and Investment, 1951–1972. In percentage of GNP*

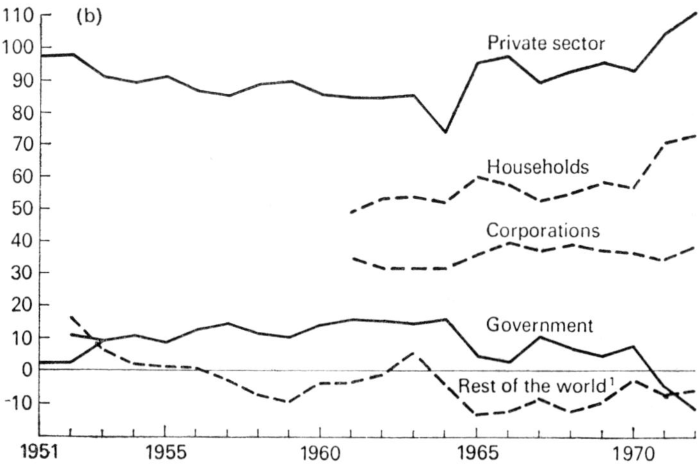

FIG. 4(*b*) *Sources of saving. In percentage of gross domestic saving*

1. Positive = deficit on current account; negative = surplus on current account.

From: O.E.C.D., *Economic Surveys, Italy* (1972); for 1972, Bank of Italy.

TABLE 7

Employment, labour force, and total population, 1960–1972, in thousands

	Changes from previous year (based on annual averages)													Absolute figures	
	1960	'61	'62	'63	'64	'65	'66	'67	'68	'69	'70	'71	'72	1959	1972
Agriculture	−280	−360	−384	−532	−355	−38	−309	−109	−307	−222	−338	−25	−290	6,847	3,298
Industry	212	258	196	151	−36	−298	−127	160	105	158	162	37	−118	7,176	8,036
Services	38	138	34	−4	235	−138	70	158	156	−125	258	−60	94	6,146	6,990
Total employment	−30	36	−154	−385	−156	−474	−366	209	−46	−189	82	−48	−314	20,169	18,331
Under-employment[1]	..	..	..	..	49	123	−229	−48	12	20	−25	61	−33	348	278
Unemployment	−281	−126	−99	−107	45	165	45	−80	5	−29	−46	—	88	1,117	697
Labour force	−311	−90	−253	−492	−111	−309	−321	129	−41	−218	36	−48	−226	21,286	19,028
Non-active population	674	279	660	865	614	710	708	308	419	552	359	401	650	27,318	34,520
Total population	363	189	407	373	503	401	387	437	378	334	395	353	424	48,609	53,548

1. Available only from 1964.

Sources: 1959 and 1960: ISTAT, *Occupati presenti in Italia* (1951–71).
1961–72: revised data supplied by ISTAT.

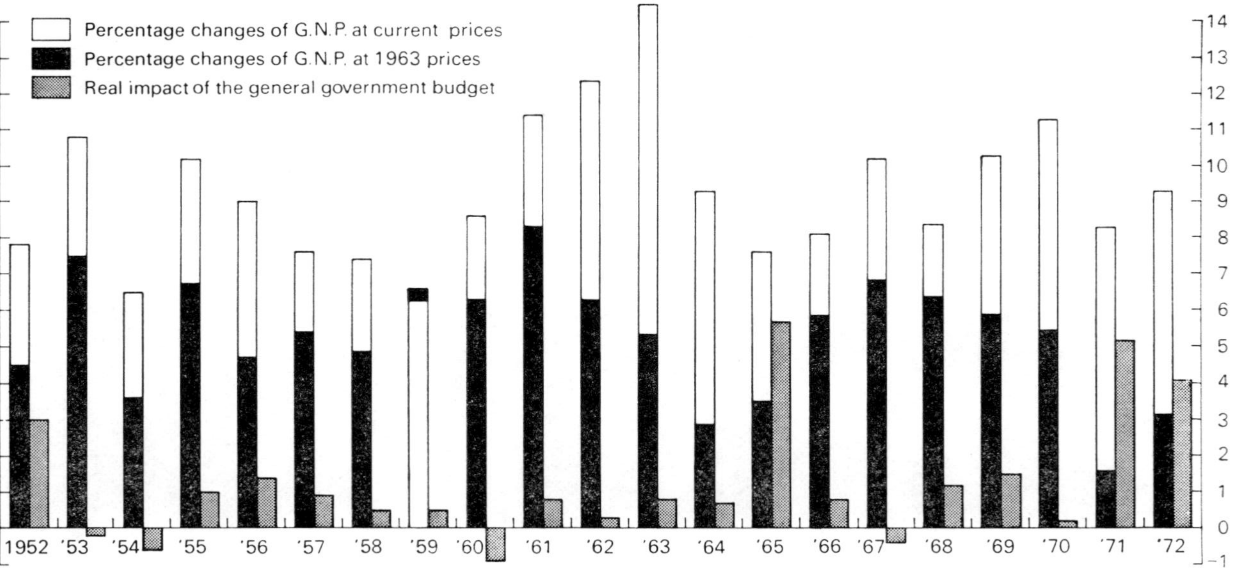

FIG. 5 *The contribution of general government to growth of GNP, 1952–1972*
Source: Bank of Italy, *Relazione Annuale*.

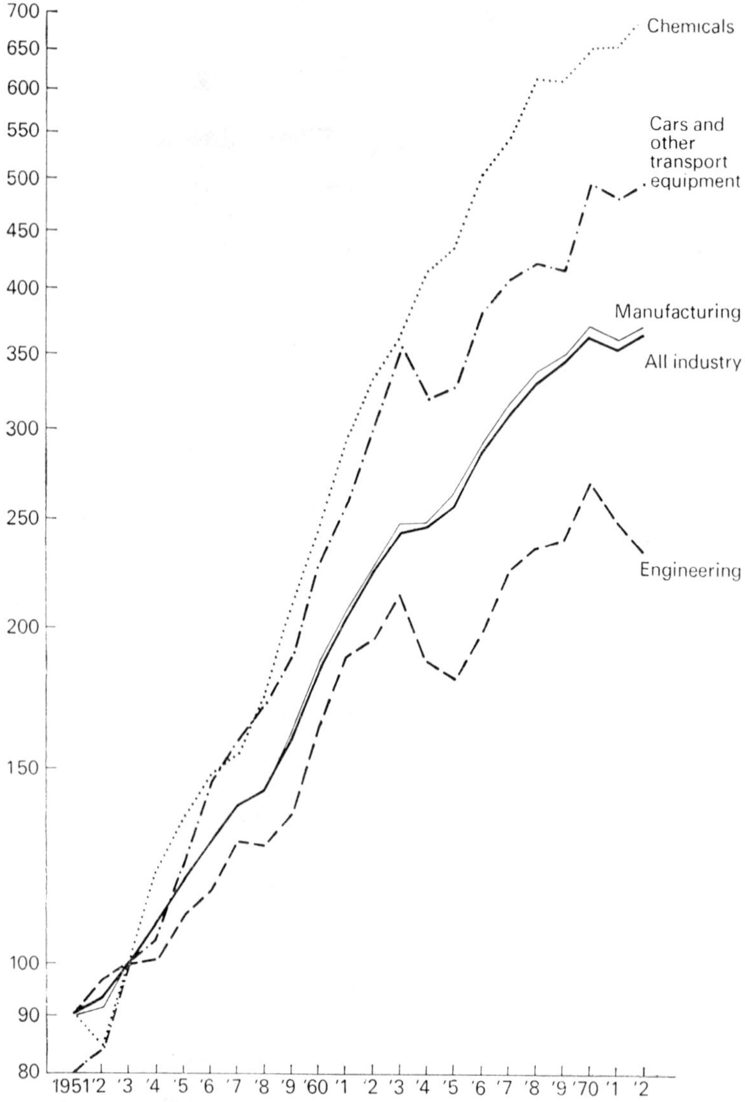

Fig. 6 *Industrial production, 1953–1972*
Indices (1953 = 100)
Source: ISTAT.

TABLE 8

Labour costs in the private sector, 1969–1972
annual percentage increases

	Output[1]	Employment	Output per man	Labour income per dependent employed	Unit labour cost
PRIVATE SECTOR TOTAL					
1969	6·3	0·4	5·8	8·6	2·6
1970	5·5	0·5	4·9	17·2	11·7
1971	1·4	−1·5	2·9	14·5	11·2
1972	3·3	−1·5	4·9	10·5	5·4
AGRICULTURE					
1969	3·0	−4·4	7·7	12·1	4·1
1970	−0·4	−7·6	7·8	16·9	8·5
1971	1·6	−4·1	5·9	18·3	11·6
1972	−4·9	−8·1	3·4	16·0	12·2
INDUSTRY					
1969	6·9	1·8	5·0	8·5	3·4
1970	6·3	2·4	3·8	18·6	14·2
1971	−0·5	−1·4	0·9	12·9	11·9
1972	3·9	−0·9	4·8	10·7	5·6
SERVICES					
1969	6·8	1·8	4·9	7·7	2·7
1970	6·6	3·1	3·4	13·9	10·0
1971	4·0	—	4·0	15·9	11·1
1972	5·5	1·4	4·0	9·0	4·8

1. Gross product at factor cost at constant prices.
Source: Bank of Italy, *Relazione Annuale*.

Table 9

General government consolidated account, 1961–1972, according to national accounts concepts billions of lira

	1961	'62	'63	'64	'65	'66	'67	'68	'69	1970	'71	'72
Direct taxes	1288	1561	1770	2084	2361	2592	2941	3210	3504	3571	4043	4870
Indirect taxes	3944	3420	3803	4146	4517	4821	5508	5912	6366	6950	7513	7967
Social security contributions	2089	2517	3208	3676	3694	3889	4594	5297	5568	6631	7376	8375
Other current receipts	652	709	797	870	977	1135	1249	1330	1570	1735	2144	2585
Total current revenue	7072	8208	9577	10776	11549	12436	14292	17749	17009	18888	21076	23798
Current expenditure on goods and services	2872	3349	4080	4594	5176	5521	5861	6382	6898	7362	8925	10134
Current subsidies and transfers	3291	3888	4543	5005	6129	6797	7553	8747	9673	10711	12637	15550
Total current expenditure	6163	7237	8624	9598	11305	12318	13415	15129	16571	18073	21562	25684
Net current savings	909	971	954	1178	244	117	877	621	438	814	−486	−1886
Depreciation allowances and capital account receipts	78	88	101	111	124	132	142	145	176	367	215	230
Gross investment	710	757	838	978	939	1014	987	1189	1215	1338	1428	1804
Capital transfers	316	324	316	335	589	548	765	755	810	1171	946	996
Change in net indebtedness	39	23	100	25	1158	1312	733	1179	1410	1328	2644	4456

Sources: ISCO, *Quadri della contabilità nazionale italiana per il periodo 1951–1971* (1972); Ministero del Bilancio, *Relazione Generale* (1972).

TABLE 10

Shares of selected items of the general government budget in GNP at current prices, 1951–2, 1961–2, and 1971–2

	1951–2	1961–2	1971–2
Direct taxes	4·1	5·5	6·7
Indirect taxes	10·6	12·5	11·7
Social Security contributions	5·3	8·9	11·9
Total current revenue	21·9	29·6	33·9
Current expenditure on goods and services	11·9	12·1	14·4
Current subsidies and transfers	9·8	13·9	21·3
Total current expenditure	21·7	26·0	35·7
Gross investment	2·5	2·8	2·4

Sources: ISCO, *Quadri della contabilità nazionale italiana per il periodo 1951–1971* (1972); Ministero del Bilancio, *Relazione Generale* (1972).

TABLE 11

The monetary base, 1961–1972
changes from previous year, in billion lira

	1962	'63	'64	'65	'66	'67	'68	'69	'70	'71	'72
CREATION											
Net impact of foreign sector	608	−718	294	627	235	243	123	−648	319	478	233
Net impact of public sector	582	979	795	932	481	405	922	1500	2991	2612	4246
Banks	271[1]	475	−164	−165	562	626	220	469	−1276	90	1435
Other sectors	−8	−7	6	−55	−39	−58	−24	−76	119	131	−42
Total	1453	729	931	1339	1239	1216	1241	1245	2153	3311	5872
USES											
Public and non-bank intermediaries	698	752	546	802	831	1017	577	1153	984	1782	3855
Credit institutions	755	−23	385	537	408	199	664	92	1169	1529	2017
Total	1453	729	931	1339	1239	1216	1241	1245	2153	3311	5872

1. Including 200 billion lire for the reduction of the coefficient of compulsory reserves.
Source: Bank of Italy.

TABLE 12

Yields of securities, 1962–1972
percentages

	Government securities	Bonds	Shares
1962	5·06	5·78	3·28
1963	5·20	6·07	3·85
1964	5·79	6·97	4·50
1965	5·42	6·67	4·57
1966	5·48	6·37	3·80
1967	5·59	6·46	4·15
1968	5·63	6·54	4·35
1969	5·81	6·73	4·01
1970	7·72	8·63	4·09
1971	7·04	8·02	4·36
1972	6·58	7·29	3·40

Source: Bank of Italy.

PART TWO

STRUCTURAL PROBLEMS AND POLICIES

CHAPTER 5

THE LABOUR MARKET

DEVELOPMENTS in the Italian labour market display a number of special features which distinguish it from that of other countries. These are illustrated in Table 7 in Part One, which presents data on changes in employment by major sectors of activity and in total employment, unemployment, under-employment, and the labour force and total population in the period 1959–72.

Throughout the period there has been a substantial decline in agricultural employment as a result of a massive outflow of population from farms to urban centres and from the South to other regions of the country, the outflow slowing down in recession years—notably in 1965, 1971, and 1972. Over the period as a whole agricultural employment fell from 6·8 million to 3·3 million persons. Employment in other sectors of activity increased (again the increase was checked or became negative in recession years) but the rise was not sufficient to absorb the manpower released from agriculture. Whereas agricultural employment declined by 3·5 million, the absorption by all other sectors amounted to only 1·7 million persons. As a consequence total employment fell by 1·8 million or 10 per cent while GNP rose by more than 90 per cent over the period. At the same time officially recorded unemployment declined by 420,000 persons and under-employment also fell.*

The total outcome of these various tendencies was a fall in the labour force (the sum of the employed and the officially recorded unemployed) by 2·2 millions and an increase in the non-active population—that is of persons who were neither

* Under-employed or marginally employed are those who work less than 33 hours a week for 'reasons of an economic character or because of a lack of a larger supply of jobs' (official definition). Official estimates of the numbers under-employed have been available only since 1964.

employed nor recorded as looking for a job—by 7·3 million persons. Since the total population rose by 4·9 million, the contraction of the labour force cannot be attributed to demographic developments.

The singularity of these tendencies becomes evident when the behaviour of activity rates (the labour force as a percentage of the population aged 15 to 64) in Italy is contrasted with that of a number of other countries (see Fig. 7). While most other countries registered only very minor changes in their activity rates between 1959 and 1970, the Italian participation rate declined from 65·4 to 55·7 per cent and to by far the lowest ratio of any of the countries shown—whether highly industrialized or less developed. Activity rates in Italy dropped further in 1971 and 1972. Expressed as a share of the total population of all ages, the rate amounted to only 35·5 per cent in 1972. This means that only a little more than one-third of the population supports, or seeks to support, through gainful employment, close to two-thirds.

The exceptionally low level of over-all activity rates is largely accounted for by the small female participation in the labour force. Measured by the ratio of the active population to the whole population, the female activity rate amounted to 25 per cent in 1970 against a male ratio of 72 per cent. In 1960, the corresponding rates had been 31·5 per cent and 81 per cent respectively. In international comparison the male participation rate ranks rather low, but for women not only is it the lowest in western Europe except for Portugal, but the distance from the next country higher up the scale is very long indeed.

A great deal has been written about the causes of these startling developments of the Italian labour market.[1] It has been argued by some that the decline in activity rates (and the huge increase in the non-active population) was largely due to 'normal factors' on the supply side, that is to the voluntary withdrawal of potential job-seekers from the labour market which is common to all developed countries. The raising of the school-leaving age and greater school-

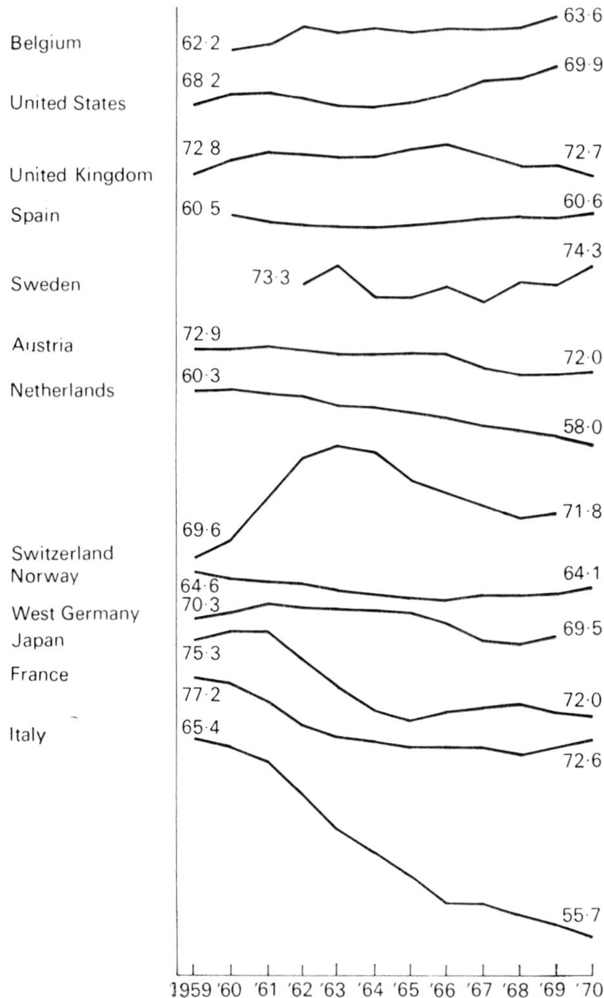

FIG. 7 *Total labour force as percentage of total population aged 15–64 in selected countries, 1959–1970*
From: O.E.C.D., *Labour Force Statistics.*

attendance reduced the entry of young people into the labour market, it is said, while the lowering of pensionable retirement age curtailed the supply of labour from the older age-groups. However, the recent tendencies for extension of school attendance beyond the official school-leaving age, as well as the growing share of first-job seekers among the unemployed, suggest that much of the non-activity among the young age-groups cannot be voluntary and that the continuation of study has served as a substitute for a job. The numbers of first-job seekers increased by 32 per cent from 1971 to 1972 and they accounted for 62 per cent of officially recorded unemployment in 1972. Among them, over 40 per cent had completed secondary schooling or held university degrees. Similarly, the low pensions paid in Italy, as well as the fact that older people often seek occasional work, support the view that the factor limiting the numbers remaining in the labour market lies on the demand rather than the supply side.

Another important cause of the rise in the non-active population was the enormous shift in the structure of output and employment away from agriculture to other sectors of activity. The outflow from agriculture and the migration to towns compelled women (as also other family-helpers in agriculture) to leave the labour market both because of limited employment opportunities in non-agricultural jobs and because family duties prevent their seeking employment outside the home. Almost one million female unpaid family-helpers left agriculture between 1960 and 1971.

Other experts support the 'discouraged worker' hypothesis, according to which workers give up even looking for a job because of weak demand for labour. They point out that it can hardly be argued that the steady decline in activity rates and their exceptionally low present level are a reflection of high incomes. Comparison of other countries rather suggests that there is no inverse relationship between participation rates and *per capita* incomes. Moreover if there were, one would expect that, within Italy, activity rates would be higher in the poor regions than in the prosperous ones; but in fact activity rates range from an average of some 41 per cent in the North to 38 per cent in the Centre and only 33 per cent in the South.

Perhaps the most convincing evidence of the existence of a vast potential labour supply scarcely reflected in official unemployment and under-employment data, and of the inability of the Italian economy, in particular the Southern region, to provide sufficient employment opportunities for its population, is supplied by large-scale emigration. Emigration from the South amounted to more than 2 million persons in the period 1951–61. The 1961 and 1971 censuses indicated that another 2,318,000 persons emigrated from the South in that decade. Of these, the North and Centre absorbed 1,161,000 while net emigration abroad amounted to 1,157,000. Thus large numbers of people, mainly in the South, were compelled to migrate in order to find a livelihood either in other areas of Italy or in foreign countries. While the migrants' economic situation improved in their new places of residence and work, they had to put up with a great deal of hardship in an environment to which they were not accustomed and which was frequently hostile. Moreover, neither in the immigration regions within Italy nor, on the whole, in other countries did the authorities provide the social infra-structures required to create decent conditions of life for the immigrants.

Thus the so-called 'normal factors' have certainly played some part in the reduction of Italian activity rates but the main explanations must be sought elsewhere. This has been partly confirmed by an inquiry held by the Statistical Institute (ISTAT) in February 1971, which showed that, out of a non-active population between the ages of 14 and 70 of 18,737,000, 18 per cent (3,370,000) expressed readiness to accept paid work on certain conditions. More than half of this group were women and most of the remainder students and pensioners. Close to 30 per cent of the 3,370,000 would be available for work only during some months of the year, the rest during either the whole or a major part of the year; 18 per cent of them declared themselves disposed to work anywhere, 25 per cent only at home, and 56 per cent near their home.

While the results of the inquiry tend to confirm the existence of a 'discouraged worker' component in the non-labour force, it is extremely difficult to draw any conclusions as to the extent of the waste of labour resources in Italy. Since the various groups answering different questions partly overlap, it is hazardous to quantify the share of hidden unemployment in the non-active population. The O.E.C.D. estimated such hidden unemployment at some 500,000, which would raise total unemployment in 1971 from 613,000 to 1·1 million persons or from 3·1 to 5·5 per cent of the labour force. However, even this adjusted figure could still not supply a satisfactory explanation of the low activity rates which distinguish Italian labour market conditions from those of other countries.

The evidence in any case suggests the existence of a large reserve of unoccupied labour, ready to work in non-agricultural activities and to transfer to other areas. The major condition for this part of the non-active population finding work is not only the creation of sufficient demand in aggregate but also an appropriate location and composition of that demand. But for a major component of the non-active population—female labour—the lack of professional training and the inadequacy or absence of social services such as nursery schools, school transport and school meals, canteens in factories, etc., also constitute major obstacles to entry into the labour force. There is also a persistent and deeply-ingrained traditional aversion to working outside the home, particularly in the backward regions, both on the part of the women themselves and of their male family members. On the demand side, a contributing factor to the decline in female activity rates has been the shrinking of handicraft activities and of the textile industry where female employment predominated.

Further light on the over-all behaviour of activity rates in the 1960s is thrown by Table 13. The decline of the male labour force has affected mainly the two extreme age-groups

TABLE 13

Specific activity rates by age-group and sex in 1960 and 1970

Age-groups	Males 1960	Males 1970	Females 1960	Females 1970
14–19	67·3	38·4	45·3	28·9
20–4	78·3	69·4	48·3	43·3
25–9	96·2	93·9	36·2	33·2
30–4	98·1	98·2	34·4	29·7
35–9	97·6	98·2	34·3	29·9
40–4	96·7	97·3	33·5	30·8
45–9	96·0	95·0	31·9	29·2
50–4	92·8	90·7	30·5	25·9
55–9	86·5	81·1	24·2	18·3
60–4	60·5	48·2	17·9	10·6
more than 65	30·0	12·9	8·5	2·6
Total	81·2	72·1	31·7	24·8

Source: ISTAT, *Annuario di Statistiche del Lavoro* (1971).

(14–24 and 55–64 years). In the middle age-brackets (30–44 years) male activity rates remained unchanged or increased and show a high ratio of around 98 per cent. The substitution, for young and old male workers, of workers in the middle age-groups reflects an increasing orientation of industrial demand for labour to the most productive, experienced, and qualified of the male working population. Activity rates for females declined in all age-groups; but here, also, the extreme age-brackets were most affected, though the highest activity rate was still found in the age-group 20–4.

All in all, there appears to have been a tendency for demand for labour to be highly selective, particularly in industry, with a preference for male workers and, among them, for the intermediate age-groups; the weaker components of the labour force—the young, old, and women—have been partly eliminated. Moreover, the demand for the stronger components of the labour force was highly concentrated in the industrial regions. These demand tendencies help to explain the apparent contradiction of weakening aggregate demand for labour in recent years and simultaneous strains in some segments of the labour market.

The structural weaknesses of the Italian labour market are particularly marked in the South. In Southern Italy and the Islands the labour force amounted to 32 per cent of the total population. The corresponding ratio in the North-West—the richest region of Italy—was 40 per cent. The figures indicate that from 1961 to 1971 labour market conditions worsened in the South in relation to those in the rest of Italy, and thus the initial comparative disadvantage of the South regarding the level and pattern of employment increased.

Percentage changes in the labour force, 1961–1971

	Centre–North	South
Employment in:		
Agriculture	−48·2	−32·0
Industry	+10·1	+0·9
Other activities	+9·8	+13·0
Total employment	−4·8	−9·5
Unemployment	−17·8	−8·0
Total labour force	−5·2	−9·5

While the share of agriculture in total employment in the South declined and that of industry increased, the former remained far above and the latter far below the corresponding shares in the Centre–North. The increase in the share of tertiary activities and public administration, as also the sharp absolute increase of employment in these sectors and the higher level of this share than in the Centre–North, reflect the failure of industry to provide sufficient employment for labour released from agriculture and for new entries into the labour market. Part of the redundant labour found employment in precarious and low-productivity activities in various service branches and handicrafts, or in an already overcrowded and inefficient bureaucracy where political considerations entered into the recruitment procedures. The rest joined the non-active population and, in more recent years, came to swell the numbers of unemployed.

Another specific aspect of Italian labour market conditions

is of interest. The size of the non-active population has been overestimated and that of the labour force underestimated to some extent because of the existence of 'hidden employment' the size of which it is difficult to ascertain. It is made up of disparate elements, such as persons doing various jobs for industrial firms at home without social security payments by the employer; pensioners who continue to work unofficially so as not to lose their pensions; students doing seasonal work and work in tourism; ex-civil servants and bank employees whose early retirement permits them to take on non-recorded employment in other occupations.

Composition of employment
Percentages

	Centre–North		South	
	1961	1971	1961	1971
Agriculture	24·9	13·5	42·6	30·9
Industry	41·8	46·6	27·7	30·4
Tertiary activities	26·7	31·1	22·1	26·9
Public administration	6·6	8·8	7·6	10·4

There is further the widespread phenomenon of double employment. This does not directly affect the recorded employment figures; but it does increase family incomes and may make it unnecessary for other family members to seek gainful employment. Thus many public employees take on jobs outside their normal working hours; an inquiry among the employees of five public institutions found that 27 per cent of the staff had a second job. In the public administration 750,000 persons out of a total of 1,800,000 have been estimated to take on secondary employment. Industrial workers have secondary activities, such as running repair shops, and peasants continue their farm labour besides being employed in other occupations.

Nevertheless, there is a considerable waste of labour resources in Italy which official unemployment and under-employment data fail to reflect; and among the registered employed there are many in precarious employment, particularly in agriculture and in services, which is characterized by instability of job and pay and is not covered by social security provisions.* The large increase and the exceptionally high level of the non-active population can be ascribed only very partially to the decline in the labour supply which is a common feature to all industrial countries. The rate of growth of demand for labour and its composition must account for a good part of it. The features of the Italian development pattern which were responsible for the insufficient mobilization of labour resources are mentioned at various points in this study: the low level of public investment expenditure; the policy-induced stagnation of investment in the labour-intensive house-building sector; the failure of development policies in the South to provide sufficient industrial employment due to the prevalence of capital-intensive investment projects; and the absence of an active labour market policy. It emerges from all this that except for purely verbal pronouncements, the problems of employment have been relegated to the field of 'non-policies'.[2]

* It will be recalled that the under-employed are defined as persons working less than 33 hours a week. However, to work the full standard working week does not preclude under-employment of a different kind.

CHAPTER 6

REGIONAL DUALISM: THE SOUTH

NEXT to the under-utilization of labour, and partly responsible for it, the under-development of the South and the large gap between the levels of development in the South and the Centre–North of Italy have been the most serious and intractable problem of the country in the post-war period. The 'Mezzogiorno' differs from depressed or backward regions in other western European countries in both quantitative and qualitative terms. It must be borne in mind that the South covers more than 40 per cent of the national territory and that it contained 36 per cent of the Italian population in 1971. It consists of the following regions: Abruzzi, Molise, Campania, Apulia, Basilicata, Calabria, and the two islands Sicily and Sardinia (see map). With almost 20 million inhabitants, it had twice the population of Belgium or Portugal and approached that of Yugoslavia.

In 1951, when policies for the promotion of economic development in the Mezzogiorno were initiated, the area had many of the features of an underdeveloped country—low *per capita* income, high unemployment and under-employment, low activity rates, a low investment ratio and low productivity, and mass emigration. Employment and output were both provided predominantly by agriculture; agriculture was characterized by archaic methods of production, and demographic pressure on poor agricultural resources was intense. The small industrial sector comprised mainly traditional and handicraft industries organized in small enterprises. Compared with industry, the tertiary sector was large; but it was made up mostly of inefficient small-scale commercial and service activities and various other precarious occupations. All sectors suffered from fragmentation and from the lack of modern techniques and equipment and of basic infra-structure. Incomes were almost completely absorbed by consumption, and inadequate local saving resulted in an excessive dependence on external funds to finance investment.

A few statistical indicators serve to illustrate some of the features of the relative underdevelopment of the South, although averages for the two parts of Italy cover up substantial differences between individual regions in each of the parts. Income per head in the South in 1951 was only 57 per cent of that of the rest of the country; employment in agriculture accounted for 57 per cent of total employment compared with 38 per cent in the Centre–North; the corresponding ratios for manufacturing were 13 and 27 per cent. Private-sector activities outside agriculture provided 38 per cent and 57 per cent of employment in the South and Centre–North respectively, and their shares in output were 63 and 81 per cent. The shares of industrial investment in total gross fixed-capital formation in the two areas were 26 per cent in the South and 42 per cent in the Centre–North.

Economic backwardness in the South was accompanied by educational and social underdevelopment—a high rate of illiteracy, high infant mortality, a shortage of social infrastructures (particularly schools), widespread persistence of semi-feudal attitudes and privileges, and the lack of an entrepreneurial class. Common also to the rest of Italy, but much more accentuated in the South, was an antiquated and slow-moving public administration with a frequent lack of qualification of persons in public office. The small size of the industrial sector meant that neither organized labour nor a modern managerial class was strong enough to exert an influence that could transform archaic attitudes and institutions, or to participate in the formulation of development objectives and policies. On the other hand, the large segment of the population employed in precarious, low-income tertiary activities, including public administration, constituted an economically insecure and politically immature and unstable element which could be easily swayed by party-political pressures. Bargaining for concessions in the distribution of public funds and other facilities found willing partners in the public administration, and graft and bribery were an acknowledged custom.

All these difficult problems had to be tackled in order to achieve one of the major post-war policy objectives of Italy —to reduce and eventually to eliminate the development gap between the two parts of the country. The name of Professor Pasquale Saraceno is closely associated with the gradual evolution of development policies in the South. He has been perhaps their most important single promoter and critic; and his contribution to the formula of state-holding companies and to the elaboration of planning concepts and practices has been equally important.

The so-called 'extraordinary intervention' for development in the South started with the creation in 1950 of the Cassa per il Mezzogiorno, a public fund which was subsequently placed under the control of the Interministerial Committee for the South, with the intention of synchronizing policies, specifically designed to promote development in that area, with other national aims and policies. In the first phase, the efforts to stimulate development in the South were concentrated almost entirely on agriculture and the creation of economic and social infra-structures. It was considered that prospects for large-scale industrial development, requiring the creation of modern, competitive industries in the area, were poor and that industrial growth and the conquest of external markets had to be left to the North, where the expansion of a dynamic, foreign-trade oriented industrial sector was already well under way. It was further hoped that some industrial development would spontaneously result from the multiplier effect of higher public expenditure and from the more favourable environment created by the new infra-structure investments. 'Thus the decisions to open the Italian economy to international economic integration, just as it had had a determining influence on the sectoral structure of Italian industry, ended up by also crystallizing its regional imbalance.'[1]

In the early years of Cassa's operations, some three-quarters of its funds were devoted to the promotion of agriculture. But it was not enough merely to provide investment finance to the sector; measures to change the institutional and social environment were also required. Thus a land reform provided for an expropriation (with compensation) of large land holdings and their allocation to peasant farmers, together with public investment in rural housing and in village infra-structures, and the provision of technical assistance. While these measures helped substantially to reduce rural unemployment, the size of the newly created farm units turned out to be generally too small for efficient operation.

To reduce disparities in the economic and social environment, most of the remainder of Cassa funds were allocated to infra-structure investments—water and electric energy, railway-lines, roads, tourism facilities, schools and hospitals. To assist industrial ventures which might be attracted by rising local income and demand and by the provision of social capital, special credit institutions were created in 1953; their task was to grant subsidized credit with the help of Cassa contributions.

A continuing large outflow of Southern labour, attracted by the rapid industrial expansion in the North and the abandonment of large areas in the South, especially in the interior, resulted in a waste of public investment in agriculture and infra-structures, and was among the factors causing a major change in development policies by about 1957, when emphasis began increasingly to be placed on direct stimulus of industrialization. A variety of measures was gradually adopted to stimulate industrial investment and employment: (*a*) The selection of growth areas and growth nuclei for the location of industrial activities; industrial areas are larger in surface and population than the nuclei, and the latter are intended for small-scale locally-based industrial activities. (*b*) The setting up of Consortia of local organs—communes, chambers of commerce, etc.—for decentralizing promotional action; these were responsible for the creation and management of the growth areas and nuclei, for drawing up development plans for them and for supplying the necessary infrastructure. (*c*) The provision of industrial incentives such as loans at subsidized interest rates, outright capital grants, tax concessions, and reduction of social security payments. (*d*) Directives to state-holding companies to locate 40 per cent of their total investments and 60 per cent of their new investments in the South, and an undertaking by the central authorities to purchase 30 per cent of their supplies and to locate 40 per cent of their investments in the area. (*e*) The Interministerial Committee was required to elaborate five-year expenditure plans, to indicate the criteria to be used in granting incentives and to report to Parliament on its activities. (*f*) Technical assistance and training were provided through the creation of an Institute for Assistance to the Development of the South (IASM) and a Training and Study Centre for the South (FORMEZ).

SVIMEZ, a research organization set up much earlier, was of considerable importance in preparing studies on the problems of the South and submitting critical evaluations of the policies pursued and results obtained.

The Cassa funds were substantially enlarged from over 2,000 billion lira in the fifteen-year period 1950–65 to 2,800 billion in the five years 1965–70; and the pattern of their use reflects the change in the emphasis of development policies. In the former period, 55 per cent were allocated to agriculture, 33 per cent to infra-structure and only 12 per cent to industry. In the more recent five-year period, industry obtained 48 per cent of total funds, the allocation to agriculture had shrunk to 17 per cent while infra-structures about maintained their share.

At first the aim of industrial policy was to create a network of small- and medium-sized enterprises and, in principle, not to provide special incentives for major projects which, it was thought, would be less labour-intensive. But policies gradually changed, partly because it was thought that as the agricultural labour surplus declined job-creation would become less urgent, but also because it was thought that a limitation of incentives to enterprises of moderate size virtually precluded the creation of new and technologically advanced industries. In any case, public corporations' investment projects could, by their very nature, be only of large dimensions. Thus, while support to large-scale ventures was at first conceded only in exceptional cases, it was subsequently granted on a case-to-case basis and the formula of 'programme-contracts' found increasing application. The latter provided for credit and tax concessions to large investment projects with, as a counterpart, certain constraints and commitments (e.g. location and type of investment) to which the firms undertaking them were subject.

What have been the results of twenty years of extraordinary intervention and the operations of the Cassa per il Mezzogiorno? Are they judged a success or failure in eliminating, or at least reducing, the gap between the levels of development in the South and the Centre–North?

Undoubtedly, conspicuous progress has been achieved in many respects; *per capita* income, gross domestic product, and industrial output in the South have grown rapidly; the share of agriculture in employment has been substantially reduced; productivity in agriculture and industry has increased fast; the profound transformation of agriculture, and the resulting rise in agricultural incomes, has widened the market for industrial products and increased local supplies for processing; large investments in infra-structures have created a basis for the diffusion of industrialization. However, despite these positive results, the development policies did not significantly narrow the gap between the South and the rest of the country. (For some illustrations of a persisting imbalance, see Table 14.) Thus income per head in the South has increased two and a half times over the period; but since it rose faster still in the Centre–North, *per capita* income in the South remained at less than 60 per cent of the Centre–North level, and that despite continuing mass emigration. Total employment and the labour force declined more sharply in the South than in the rest of Italy and unemployment was reduced less. The index of Southern industrial output rose to 380 (1951 = 100) but the pace of expansion was somewhat faster in the Centre–North. As to changes in the pattern of employment, the number of persons occupied in agriculture declined even more sharply in the other regions than in the South (see Chapter 5). While employment in industry rose more rapidly in the South than elsewhere, this was entirely accounted for by construction, and the rate of manpower absorption by manufacturing lagged far behind. The increase in industrial employment by 45 per cent appears all the more limited if confronted with a more than seven-fold rise in industrial investment. Next to construction, employment in services and public administration registered the most rapid

TABLE 14

Indicators of regional differences

	All Italy = 100				1951 = 100	
	South		Centre–North		South	Centre–North
	1951	1971	1951	1971	1971	
Per capita income	67·9	64·3	119·0	119·6	253·7	270·4
GDP at factor cost	24·5	22·9	75·5	77·1	272·2	298·5
Agriculture	38·6	42·6	61·4	57·4	174·8	148·1
Industry	17·0	16·6	83·0	83·4	380·7	391·9
Services	22·7	23·5	77·3	76·5	299·1	285·2
Employment[1]	33·0	34·3	66·7	65·7	91·8	101·8
Agriculture	42·6	50·4	57·4	49·6	50·0	36·5
Industry	22·5	23·2	77·5	76·8	145·2	139·3
Manufacturing	19·5	17·6	80·5	89·4	122·0	138·0
Construction	32·3	40·0	67·7	60·0	209·5	149·7
Services (private sector)	27·4	27·8	72·6	72·2	142·2	138·8
Public administration	33·3	34·3	66·7	65·7	163·4	156·3
Industrial investment outlays	15·1	35·4	84·9	64·6	732·3	239·2

1. Employment data have been adjusted after the census results of 1971. The new series is not yet available by regions.
Source: Data supplied by the Comitato dei Ministri per il Mezziogiorno.

absolute and relative expansion. While employment in industry increased by 590,000 persons, the private service sectors and public administration absorbed an additional 715,000 persons. Thus over half of the increase in non-agricultural employment was accounted for by private and public service activities. Employment increases have thus been concentrated on low-productivity sectors while value added per worker employed grew less in the South than in the Centre–North in both agriculture and industry.

What have been the causes of the only partial success of the development policies for the South and, in particular, of the failure of a substantial investment effort to set off a self-sustaining industrial development process? The view is held by some that not enough time has yet elapsed for all these investments to bear fruit in terms of a spiral of industrialization. But some of the major causes can be found in the industrial dualism which has developed *within* the South because of the co-existence of a few giant enterprises, mainly in heavy industry, with a myriad of small and inefficient enterprises. The South still does not have an integrated, interacting industrial system.

Industrial growth in the first phase was concentrated on large ventures in basic sectors such as steel (Taranto), oil-refining (Gela and Siracusa in Sicily), and chemicals (Gela, Ferrandino, and Ragusa in Sicily), which required very substantial capital outlays and were largely undertaken by public corporations. At the same time the investment efforts of the public corporations also established some of the infra-structures needed to provide the region with essential services and to create more favourable conditions for private industrial activities.

In a second phase, which is still under way, the earlier ventures in basic sectors have been further developed and new ones added—through investments in petrochemicals (Brindisi), aluminium (Sardinia), and electrometallurgy (Sicily)—some of which extended into the processing of base materials. This action has been supplemented by investments in manufacturing, with the establishment of the Alfa Sud motor-car plant near Naples and of aeronautics and food-processing industries; and a decision to locate Fiat and Pirelli factories in the South followed the founding of Alfa Sud. Investment in transport infra-structure—maritime and air transport—became important and helped to link the South more closely to other regions.

So far, however, these ventures have made a relatively small contribution to stimulating an industrial take-off. In the first place, they could directly create only a limited number of new jobs since most of the lines of production selected were highly capital-intensive. In the second place, these enterprises were largely created by groups from outside the region, predominantly state-holding companies, which remained closely tied to their central seat in the North and did not integrate with the local environment. These 'ships' or 'cathedrals in the desert', as they came to be described, relied upon imported techniques and supplies and were largely run by managers and operated by technical personnel brought in from outside. Individual personnel often stayed only for limited periods of time, being then succeeded by new drafts from outside the region. These enterprises thus not only failed to stimulate the creation of a network of subsidiary and complementary minor industries—which had been hoped for—but they remained largely peripheral to the social, cultural, and political life of the South. This 'social absenteeism' meant that

> the few regions of the South which have seen the establishment of some conspicuous industrial groups and the creation around them of groups of minor enterprises—that is, the only industrialized areas of the South (the zone Naples–Salerno, the triangle Bari–Brindisi–Taranto, and the area between Catania and Siracusa) have enjoyed the benefits of industrialization only in the form of growth of income and employment, without receiving a parallel stimulus to the development of social life to standards more adapted to the requirements of modern society.[2]

Although a large number of relatively small enterprises have also been created, or kept alive, with the help of various incentives, many other small and handicraft enterprises have disappeared, with resulting large losses of employment. The publicly supported small and medium-sized firms have suffered from insufficient external economies, shortages of skilled labour and modern entrepreneurship, and from the lack of local savings. They have been further handicapped by insufficient access to technical assistance and know-how, which in the North is often provided to similar enterprises through their connections with large firms, in the form of advice on technical innovation, specialization, market prospects, and sales promotion. The effects of special incentives have thus not been sufficient to transform the greater part of the numerous inefficient and non-competitive firms into modern industrial units, or even to preserve many of them from extinction.

Moreover, no adequate criteria have been established for the allocation of subsidies, either by the public authorities or the specialized credit institutions. This failure brought into play the usual mechanism of arbitrary decisions based on political favouritism and bureaucratic manoeuvring, with all the well-known accompanying ill-effects of long delays and a misallocation and waste of resources.

Other defects in the industrial policies in the South stem from the insufficient co-ordination between industrial, urban, and infra-structure development within the area and the absence of any clear concept of an industrial policy for the country as a whole. Regarding the former, part of the outflow from agriculture went to towns *within* the South, and resulted in excessive urban concentrations offering only limited industrial employment. The majority of the new populations of the towns therefore drifted into various service occupations of a precarious nature or joined the non-active population, subsisting on occasional work and sporadic income. Moreover, the lack of social services and urban equipment in the rapidly growing agglomerations created conditions of life which are intolerable by western European standards. Some sections of Naples and Palermo, for instance, give an alarming visual impression of these deficiencies; and the spotlight turned on some Southern cities as a result of the cholera outbreak in September 1973 revealed a shocking deterioration in the hygienic and general environmental conditions.

The absence of a clearly conceived and co-ordinated industrial policy resulted in contradictory policy measures, some of which partially or wholly offset incentives specifically designed to promote industrial development in the South. It was not sufficiently realized that many activities in the Mezzogiorno could only be developed in substitution for, and not as additions to, similar activities in the Centre–North. Thus provisions to assist small- and medium-sized industries were applied to the whole national territory without appropriate discrimination in favour of the South; some measures to assist depressed regions also covered the Centre–North, and the same applies to operations to rescue industries in chronic difficulties, such as textiles and shipbuilding.

Among other recent obstacles to a more rapid and widespread industrial development of the South have been the rise of labour costs and their progressive equalization between the South and the rest of the country. This reduced one of the major incentives for locating new investments in the South and narrowed the margins within which investment subsidies could compensate for location disadvantages. It also provided a stimulus to productivity-raising and labour-saving, rather than to labour-intensive, investments. Furthermore, price and cost increases reduced the real effect of the financial assistance granted to new projects. The recent recession and cost inflation has had a particularly adverse effect on the profitability of small and medium-sized enterprises in the whole of Italy; but the predominance of such enterprises in the South has meant that the Southern economy was even more severely hit, and a large number of minor firms which had been in more or less chronic difficulties have been eliminated.

The overwhelming dependence of the South on public support and public initiatives meant that the deficiencies of the system regulating public expenditure caused more serious loss of potential benefits here than in other regions. Excessive delays in the decision-making process and in the execution of public expenditure projects, and the tendency for public spending to be increasingly concentrated on current rather than investment outlays have meant that consumer income was favoured at the expense of the creation of productive capacities, and also that 'income distribution' was shifted 'in favour of those groups which administer the flow of public expenditure'.[3]

Moreover, the South was increasingly subject to competition for public funds from the rest of the country. Large-scale immigration and urbanization, as well as the pressing claims of trade unions for better social welfare provisions, produced enormous increases in current public expenditure—both social transfer payments and public wages and salaries—in the industrial triangle in the North (Lombardy, Piedmont, and Liguria). The dual character of the Italian economy was thus reflected in the competitive claims on public expenditure of social welfare objectives in the Centre–North and of investment and development objectives in the South, with the Centre–North being able to exert better-organized and more powerful pressures. It was only recently that the trade unions inscribed the acceleration of development in the South among their priority claims.

To remedy some of the qualitative defects in the development policies for the South, new legislation was passed in 1971. The institutional framework was changed by suppressing the Interministerial Committee for the South and by shifting the planning and co-ordination functions to the Interministerial Committee for Economic Planning (CIPE), so as to insert action in favour of the South into the wider framework of national planning. Authority in matters of agricultural development and the growth areas and nuclei was transferred from the Cassa per il Mezzogiorno to the Regions, while the Cassa was given responsibility for the so-called 'Special Projects'.

Specific new provisions were the legal recognition of the principle of extending incentives already available to small- and medium-sized enterprises to cover selected major projects as well; a special reduction of social security contributions to offset the disappearance of pay differentials between North and South; and the raising of public corporation investment targets in the South from 40 per cent to 60 per cent of their aggregate investment outlays and from

60 per cent to 80 per cent of their outlays on new projects.

But the most important innovation was the institution of a new system of 'Special Projects', intended as an instrument for changing the quality and composition of investment and for co-ordinating the timing, dimensions, and location of related projects. The increase of employment opportunities and further structural change are their major objectives. 'Special Projects' are to make a four-pronged attack on the imbalances in Southern development—through the creation of general infra-structures, a better utilization of local natural resources and safeguard of the environment, the equipment of metropolitan areas and of new development zones, and the promotion of productive activities with the help of interrelated and integrated programmes. Compared with past policies, the main new emphasis is on planning and co-ordination, geared to precise policy objectives. The whole system of intervention now consists of two parts: the Special Projects for the intensification and co-ordination of action in a number of related fields and—side by side, and complementary, with them—the ordinary activities undertaken by the central and local authorities, the public corporations' activities, the programme-contracts for large private enterprises and the incentives to small- and medium-sized firms.

However, a successful operation of the new institutional machinery and its instruments requires as a basic precondition the existence of an operative national and regional planning system, capable of formulating and implementing central and regional objectives and policies. As we shall see, these conditions have not yet been attained.

A number of other requirements for an effective development drive in the South were listed by the present Minister of the Budget and Economic Planning shortly before his nomination. Among them is the need to eliminate various inconsistencies between national and Southern policies; to limit investment incentives to those projects which make a major contribution to growth and the creation of an industrial base, and to reduce to a minimum all incentives to sectors with high capital-intensity; to link the public corporations' obligations to locate a specified share of their investments in the South not only with capital inputs but also with the creation of jobs; and to transfer the social security contributions at present made by Southern enterprises entirely to the budget. He suggested that only such radical measures could bring about the required change in the structure of investment and make location factors in the South sufficiently favourable to promote widespread industrial development and ensure substantial increases in industrial employment. The Minister also stressed the need to link new industrial ventures to the existing network of minor or handicraft industries and to involve wide social strata in the industrialization process.

> Otherwise we shall have, as has almost always been the case, industrialization without development—that is the transfer of large Northern industry and of public enterprises to regions considered peripheral, where the location of some productive capacity may be convenient but where they make no contribution through participation in the social, cultural and political life.[4]

One major factor has to be taken into account: the closer contact with the rest of the country and with other industrialized areas brought about by improved transport, mass media, and returning migrants, has made the inhabitants of the South increasingly aware of the conditions of life, levels and patterns of consumption, and social relationships prevailing in more advanced societies. This has led to a growing intolerance of present conditions and a refusal to accept any further postponement of the social and economic unification of the country. This impatience has found expression in political extremism and in outbursts of violence, introducing a new element of urgency into the problems of the Mezzogiorno.

CHAPTER 7

PUBLIC CORPORATIONS

PUBLIC corporations or state-holding companies constitute, in principle, a powerful instrument for economic management and the implementation of economic plans in Italy, through the influence the authorities are able to exercise on the level and the sectoral and regional distribution of the corporations' investments.[1] Both the size and the range of activity of the public corporations have grown enormously in the post-war period. The system of public ownership of shareholdings in private firms started as an emergency operation in the depression of the 1930s, when three banks (Banca Commerciale Italiana, Credito Italiano, and Banco di Roma) got into financial difficulties and IRI (Istituto per la Riconstruzione Industriale) was created to take over both the industrial shareholdings owned by these banks and control of the banks themselves. IRI steadily enlarged and diversified its field of activity, operating through financial holding companies which group and control a wide range of industrial and service enterprises. Among the many sectors in which IRI operates through holding companies are iron and steel (Finsider), metal works (Finmeccanica), shipbuilding (Fincantieri), shipping (Finmare), and telecommunications (STET). IRI has under its direct control air transport (Alitalia), radio and television (RAI), four banks—the Banco di Santo Spirito was added to the original three banks—and a mixed bag of manufacturing industries and services (SME), lately operating mainly in the food sector. If all these activities are considered in the aggregate, IRI becomes the second-largest giant concern in Europe and accounts for 71 per cent of total investment outlays by public corporations in Italy in 1971.

In 1953 ENI (Ente Nazionale Idrocarburi), another public corporation, was created for the hydrocarbon sector.

It subsequently extended its activities to engineering, petrochemicals, nuclear energy, textiles, and some service industries; and ENI accounted for another 18 per cent of state-holding company investment in 1971.

EFIM (Ente Partecipazione a Finanziamento Industria Manufattureira) has two purposes—to create some basic industries which were practically non-existent in Italy, such as non-ferrous metals, and to contribute to the absorption of unemployed labour and the conversion and restructuring of companies in a number of industrial and service branches. Two minor public corporations manage spas and operate in the cinema industry. Finally, in 1971 EGAM (Ente Autonomo di Gestione per le Aziende Minerarie Metallurgiche) and GEPI (Gestione Partecipazione Industriali) were set up, the former to help overcome the crisis of the minerals and metals sector and the latter to assist industries which find themselves in special difficulties.

One of the features which distinguish the system of state-holding companies from the outright nationalizations carried out in other countries is that the latter have usually occurred in basic sectors, whereas the state-holding companies have entered a wide range of manufacturing and services, thus exercising a growth-initiating and diversifying, as well as a growth-sustaining, function. Another is that state-holding companies generally do not control the whole sector in which they operate and that individual public corporations generally own less than the total share capital of a particular company, often quite substantially less. It has been stressed by Stuart Holland that the multi-sectoral character of the state-holding companies and their only partial control of the activities in each sector influence the investment behaviour of the competing private companies in the sector. The public authorities, by using

> a multi-sectoral package of State firms in the main manufacturing branches as spearheads or pace-setters for the private firms with which they compete . . . can thereby contribute to ensuring a broad wave of investment throughout manufacturing as a whole.[2]

Public corporations are not intended to suspend the

market mechanism. They are supposed to gear the operation of market forces to the broader objectives of government policy and to act as a complement to the private sector in fields where the latter cannot be expected to provide solutions to longer-term structural problems, such as chronic national or regional unemployment or stagnating investment. They are intended particularly to guard against neglect of slow-maturing projects requiring substantial capital outlays which may be unattractive to private industry.

Public corporations exercise their influence not only quantitatively—by raising the total volume of investment—but also qualitatively—by influencing its pattern and location to meet national policy aims. Emphasis has also been placed on their role in developing high-level managerial capacities and in acting as spearheads for technical innovation.

The Minister for State Participation, who is charged with the implementation of investment programmes formulated by the Interministerial Committee for Economic Planning, has listed the following objectives for the operations of state-holding companies: to provide an impetus to the growth of sectors which have substantial short- or long-run influence on the rate of expansion of the economy; to orient their activities towards the depressed regions and to link sectoral expansion with the improvement of regional economic and social structures; to satisfy the basic needs for services, with a view to achieving higher living standards; to counteract the negative effects of oligopolistic practices in certain sectors; and to reorganize sectors whose structure no longer meets the changed requirements of the economy. In broader terms, public corporations should be an instrument for the achievement of the over-all economic and social objectives of government policies within a framework of economic and social planning.

Profit remains one of the objectives of the managers of public corporations, to provide a stimulus to efficiency and a rational allocation of resources. But the profit motive has to be combined with and modified by the criterion of maximum net social benefit (i.e. contribution to national economic and social objectives). Moreover, the profit criterion on which investment decisions are partly based differs from that of most private firms in that it applies to returns over a longer time-period than is normally taken into account by private industry.

The organizational structure of public corporations is on three levels: at the top the public authorities formulate, in accordance with over-all objectives, the general policy lines to be pursued. At the bottom of the pyramid, individual enterprises operate according to enterprise criteria of efficiency and profitability. In between, the holding company exercises a mediatory function by influencing the choice of entrepreneurial policies best suited both for carrying out the directives from the top and also for safeguarding the efficiency of the enterprise. Individual enterprises, however, maintain their day-to-day autonomy *vis-à-vis* the holding company and the latter *vis-à-vis* the public authorities. Directives and controls from the top relate primarily to decisions on entry into new sectors and financing through state funds. There are no specific directives on the location, dimension, or type of production of the public corporations, except within the framework of 'programme-contracts' freely entered into by the latter; but there is a constant exchange of views under the stimulus, orientation, and co-ordination of the Ministry.

The growing importance of public corporations in the Italian economy can be gauged from a number of indicators. Their role as an instrument of short-term demand management has already been referred to in Part One; and Fig. 3 showed that, while investment by public corporations had behaved pro-cyclically in the past, particularly in the 1964–5 recession, it became a strong counter-cyclical support to investment activity when private capital expenditure sharply declined in the recent recession. As regards their longer-term impact, the share of *all* public enterprises in total industrial investment has risen from 19 per cent in 1961 to 49 per cent in 1972. These include, in addition to the public corporations, the Electricity Agency (ENEL) since the 1963 nationalization of electricity production, and Autonomous State Agencies such as railways, ANAS (road construction), Post Office, Telephones, etc. Public corporations alone raised their share in total gross fixed investment from 8·5 per cent to 14·1 per cent in the same period; and in industry alone their share rose from 16 to 31 per cent, and in services from 13 to 17 per cent. Public corporations' investment was the only objective set for the public sector which was achieved, both as to size and composition. On the other hand, their share in total non-agricultural employment has reached only some 4 per cent, reflecting the high capital-intensity of their activities. Their capital-intensive character is further borne out by the fact that the capital stock per worker employed in public corporations was five and a half times that of industry as a whole at the end of the 1960s.

As to the pattern of public corporations' investment outlays, industry accounted for 59 per cent of the total in 1971 and services for 41 per cent. In the industrial sector, 31 per cent was absorbed by base metals, followed by mechanical industries and shipbuilding with 12 per cent, and chemicals (including petrochemicals) with 6 per cent. In service activities, telecommunications accounted for 19 per cent of total public-corporation investment and motor-ways for over 8 per cent.

To assist in the promotion of industrialization in the South has become a major function of the state-holding companies; and the sectors in which they operate, and the impact they were able to make on the industrial development of the area, have been described in the preceding chapter. Their target for investment in the South set by the law of 1957 has been surpassed; the share of total public-corporation investment located in the South rose from a 27 per cent average (excluding electricity) in 1959–62 to 46 per cent in 1968–71 and increased further to 56 per cent in 1972. In the same period the share of the South in total investment by all *other* enterprises increased from over 20 per cent to less than 30 per cent. The contribution of public corporations to total investments in the South rose from 15 per cent to 26 per cent; but their share in employment in the region increased from 3 per cent to only 4·3 per cent, again indicating the predominantly capital-intensive nature of their activities.[3]

Public corporations have thus undoubtedly played an important part in stimulating the growth of incomes, industrial production, and productivity in the South; but the direct effect of their investment on employment was very moderate. Their inherent characteristics prevented their directly stimulating the creation of private medium- and small-sized enterprises or industries, upon which widespread industrial development and much of the provision of larger employment opportunities in the South must depend.

The pattern of financing of the investment outlays of public corporations differs in many respects from that of private enterprises (see Table 15). Self-financing has accounted for a much smaller, and sharply declining, share of the total. It amounted to about one-quarter of aggregate finance in the early 1960s, rose to 45 per cent in 1968 and 1969, and dropped to 19 per cent in 1971. Apart from rising costs which affected all enterprises, the decline can be explained by the rapid increase in the volume of slow-maturing investments in the total and the obligation to locate a large proportion of their investment projects in the South where returns are relatively low. These longer-term tendencies, as well as the recent recession, have been reflected in a sharp decline in public corporations' profits.

Sources of financing specific to public corporations are the state endowment funds, which are considered as taking the place of risk-capital which would not be available from private sources for certain types of projects. They are either interest-free or require a very low return and are granted for the achievement of objectives 'in the public interest'. The size of these 'endowment funds' has usually been considered rather low by both foreign and some Italian commentators but their share in total financing has recently risen to close to one-quarter.

The major part of the investment finance needed by

public corporations is collected on financial markets. Share issues play a negligible role and financing through bond issues has become negative (repayments exceeding new issues), partly because subsidized credit is linked to borrowing from special credit institutions thus rendering the latter source of finance more attractive. An already excessive reliance on these institutions will be further accentuated by the less favourable fiscal treatment of bond issues by public

TABLE 15

Public corporations' investment outlays and their financing in 1962 and 1971

(*percentage composition*)

	1962	*1971*
Fixed investment	87·2	80·1
Other investment	12·8	19·9
Total need for finance	100·0	100·0
Self-financing	29·8	18·7
Government grants	7·6	23·0
Other external finance	62·5	58·3
Capital market	13·2	0·8
Share issues	6·2	1·5
Bond issues	7·0	−0·7
Medium- and long-term loans	25·6	34·7
Short-term credit	23·5	22·4
Other	—	0·4

Source: Ministero delle Partecipazioni Statali, *Relazione Programmatica* (1973).

corporations foreseen in the tax reform. Finally, the high share of short-term indebtedness reflects the growing preference of the public for holding their financial assets in liquid form, and the lack of financial intermediaries capable of transforming this category of savings into long-term finance for productive investment. This involves 'much greater risks and much more difficult control, as has been demonstrated by the events of long ago which were the origin of the system of State-holdings'.[4]

The important function public corporations have performed

in Italy, both as an instrument for demand management and as a weapon for structural change, could hardly be contested. The Italian experience with state-holding companies has also aroused a great deal of interest abroad, and agencies of a similar, although much more limited, character have been set up in a number of other countries. Recently, however, a growing number of spokesmen, representing widely divergent viewpoints and interests, have expressed alarm over what they consider to be a serious degeneration of the role and functioning of state-holding companies in Italy. These range from Guido Carli, the Governor of the Bank of Italy, to Antonio Giolitti, the Socialist Minister of the Budget and Economic Planning in a previous and the present Centro-Sinistra Government, and include a number of leading economists of varied political allegiance.

The vast expansion of public-corporation activities in recent years has helped to fill a vacuum left both by private sector and by general government investment. But the greater the size of the public-corporation sector, the more important becomes the establishment of, and adherence to, clearly defined investment criteria within a wider framework of longer-term planning. In fact, however, it appears that the recent expansion of public-corporation investment and the increasing recourse to financing through public endowment funds occurred without an adequate control of their investment projects being exercised either in the interests of enterprise efficiency or profitability or in that of the desired longer-term allocation of resources.

> If there has been a category of State intervention which produces distortions, it is that exercised by the supply of endowment funds to public agencies. As the volume of these funds increases, their negative effect is twofold: a parameter for the evaluation of management efficiency has been eliminated and an incentive has been provided for operating so as to produce deficits.[5]

It is true, as was pointed out by the Minister of State Participations, that it is difficult to distinguish between low returns to, or net losses from, a given investment outlay deriving from the pursuit of over-all economic and social objectives, on the one hand, and those which are caused by errors in enterprise management, on the other. But it is equally true that the rescue action public corporations performed during the recent industrial recession, in keeping alive their own deficit activities (for instance, passenger shipping) and in taking over a large number of private companies which operated at a loss (particularly in metal-working, shipbuilding, and textiles) 'without a coherent line of economic policy, leads to a degeneration of public and private entrepreneurship'.[6] These rescue operations partly reflected a policy aiming to safeguard employment opportunities, through increasing capital and labour mobility and an active labour policy; and public-corporation profits declined more than those of the large private companies. Thus gross profits of a sample of forty-seven public corporations were halved between 1969 and 1971 while those of a sample of 199 large private companies declined by 40 per cent from their 1968 peak to 1971.[7]

Another aspect of the deterioration of public-corporation operations concerns the quality and political independence of their managers. In the recruitment of managers for the public sector

> the circle of eligible citizens tends to become restricted to militants of political parties of the majority, and in this way a bureaucratized entrepreneurship is created which has but limited leanings towards innovation. The extension of the public sphere ends up by favouring the groups which can more easily bend the discretionary power of the executive to their own ends.[8]

Thus, as also in many other spheres of the economic life of the country, an originally sound and ingenious policy instrument has been weakened and distorted—one may hope only temporarily—because of the absence of an over-all industrial policy concept, the obstacles in the way of implementing planning objectives in general, and, resulting from all this, an arbitrary exercise and interplay of political and economic power.

CHAPTER 8

STRUCTURAL REFORMS

SOME of the problem areas in which structural reforms have long been considered urgent, if serious economic and social imbalances are to be corrected and the administrative and institutional framework of the Italian economic system improved, have already been mentioned in various contexts. The major reform issues can be broadly grouped as follows: town planning and transport, with particular reference to housing; health; education; agriculture; retail distribution; taxation and the budget; central and regional public administration, and, finally, methods, procedures, and institutions for over-all economic planning. The fiscal reform and the need for changes in the budget system and procedures have already been discussed in Part One. A reform of the educational system has been one of the major issues in the reform campaign, and is a basic condition for a transformation of Italian society. But the problems connected with it are complex and go far beyond the 'economic' sphere; and it will not be discussed here.

In some areas reform is already under way or appears imminent, with legislation already passed or promised; other reforms are still only at the project stage or under preliminary discussion. On the whole, much less has been done than was envisaged by the First Economic Plan for 1966–70 or than has been promised by successive governments; and obstacles at all stages of the reform process have turned out to be more difficult to surmount than was anticipated. Opposition has made itself felt all along the way, both within the public administration itself and on the part of group interests whose position was threatened by the proposed changes.* Further

* See P. Sylos-Labini, 'Sviluppo Economico e Classi Sociali in Italia', *Quaderni di Sociologia*, no. 4 (1972), for a fascinating interpretation of economic and social developments in terms of attitudes and influences of social classes,

obstruction came from delays in the execution of approved investment programmes, either because of procedural bottlenecks and/or because of insufficient financial provisions. And underlying the partial or total failure, so far, of most reform programmes, has been the antiquated, rigid, and inefficient public administration which has not been adapted to the growing responsibilities of a modern society.

Among the most flagrant structural imbalances which have emerged during Italy's rapid transformation process was the inadequate allocation of resources to social expenditure, for the satisfaction of such collective needs as housing, health, transport and education services, which had grown substantially with the large shifts of population and rapid urbanization. Despite growing needs, the rate of increase of public civil consumption expenditure slowed down in the later 1960s and its share in GNP during 1965–71 was no greater than during 1959–64. The falling off of public social investment expenditure, particularly for housing, was much more striking still.

Social expenditure at constant prices

Percentages

	Annual rates of change			Shares in GNP		
	1952–8	1959–64	1965–71	1952–8	1959–64	1965–71
Gross public consumption	4·0	5·0	3·9	11·6	10·8	10·2
Social investment	9·2	8·2	0·9	6·7	8·0	7·5
of which:						
Public administration	7·3	7·5	3·0	1·5	1·7	1·6
Housing	15·1	8·4	0·4	5·2	6·3	5·9
Total social expenditure	7·0	6·3	2·7	18·3	18·8	17·7

From: O.E.C.D., *Economic Surveys, Italy* (1972).

It has already been pointed out that the failure to accelerate expenditure on collective needs has been one of the factors in the social unrest and all-pervading disillusionment with the public authorities which have characterized the economic,

in particular the rapid growth of the lower middle class. It also provides explanations for the resistance to reforms from those groups which enjoy the greatest privileges and have the greatest power to influence political choices.

social, and political climate in recent years. Pressure for higher wages to compensate for the inadequate provision of collective services has certainly been a major element in the cost inflation.

Only a few of the reform issues and programmes have been singled out for relatively detailed treatment here; but they can serve as an illustration of the difficulties encountered by all of them.

(i) HOUSING

One of the major problem areas of Italian economic and social management in recent years has been the housing sector. Investment in residential construction expanded very rapidly in the 1950s and early 1960s, it was much less affected by the 1964 and 1965 recession than other categories of investment, and there was a renewed house-building boom in 1968 and 1969. But this boom was produced by legislation in preparation for a housing reform and was followed by a sharp decline of investment in dwellings in 1970 and 1971 and only a very slight upturn in 1972. The share of investment in dwellings in GNP amounted to 5·8 per cent in 1961, rose to 6·9 per cent in 1969 and fell again to 5·1 per cent in 1972. In international comparison of resources devoted to housing construction, Italy comes out rather well. In 1970 the ratio of investment in dwellings to GNP was 3·1 per cent in the United Kingdom, 5·3 per cent in Germany, 6·5 per cent in France, and 6·0 per cent in Italy.

The problem of the supply of housing thus stems not so much from failure to devote current resources to this purpose on a scale commensurate with other European countries as from (*a*) the extremely low standards of the past which now have to be raised (census data for years around 1960 show Italy with the largest number of persons per room among the industrial western European countries) and (*b*) the composition of housing investment. There has been a marked tendency for an increase of investment in larger-sized or luxury constructions for higher-income groups while low-cost housing has been sadly neglected. The average lire-investment per dwelling has increased, and new construction of low-cost housing has formed a declining share of total investment in dwellings. At the same time the demand for such housing became increasingly pressing as a result of the massive migrations from the South to urban concentrations in the North but also to southern towns where large numbers released from rural occupations found jobs, mainly in services and public administration. The scarcity of building sites in the cities and the absence of adequate provisions for urban and commuter transport led to real-estate speculation and to increases in the prices of urban housing far exceeding the rises in building costs. As a result the lower-income groups have had to devote an excessive share of their incomes to housing; and uncontrolled building activity has led to over-crowding, traffic congestion, the destruction of green zones and historical buildings, and a shocking scarcity of parks and sports grounds.

To counteract these tendencies, public planning and financing of low-cost housing in conjunction with town-planning measures would have been required. Instead there has been a marked long-term tendency for the share of public investment in total housing investment to decline. This was over 14 per cent in the period 1956–60, fell to 6·1 per cent in 1961–5, and from 1970 to 1972 it averaged only 3·7 per cent. Private dwelling construction has been subject to regulations administered by local authorities which have left ample scope for political and administrative pressures and electoral blackmail. 'In this sector the suspicions of collusion between the public administration and private interests have perhaps been better founded than in any other.'[1]

The history of housing legislation provides one of the most vivid illustrations of the difficulties which beset the turning of legal provisions into effectively functioning operational instruments in Italy. There have been four major steps: a town-planning law adopted as far back as August 1942; a law of April 1962 to favour the acquisition of building areas for low-cost and social housing; a law of August 1967 which modified and integrated previous provisions; and, finally, the housing reform of October 1971. It would take up too much space and time to follow this process through all its various stages. The peculiar impact of the 1967 legislation ('legge ponte') has already been mentioned (see Chapter 2). Let us then consider only the most recent reform. Its objectives were: first, to adapt the supply of housing to meet the demands, in particular, of low-income families, within a framework of physical and economic planning; second, to organize public action according to criteria governing dwelling construction as a whole, to ensure continuity in the provision of housing, and to promote technological progress in house-building; third, to ensure planning and institutional co-ordination in the short and long run between decisions on the location of productive investment and infra-structures and those on housing programmes, particularly with respect to regional distribution; fourth, to reduce obstacles to the provision of adequate housing and, specifically, speculation in real estate.

To help achieve these objectives the law provides for an expropriation by the communes of 60 per cent of scheduled building areas (sufficient to cover the estimated housing needs for a decade) at prices payable for agricultural land; and on the remaining 40 per cent construction will be authorized without specific project-by-project approval only after the establishment of an over-all urban plan, of detailed and specific area plans and of lotting projects.

The reform also provides for a radical change in the institutional framework for the housing sector. In the past, social housing was handled by a number of public agencies and finance was raised by social contributions withheld from workers' pay. The funds collected in this way were frequently not fully spent and the multiplicity of administrative and executive organs rendered procedures costly and slow. This system was to be suppressed by the end of 1973, and the various functions of planning, allocation of finance, and execution were to be divided between the central authorities, the regions and communes, and regional Autonomous

Institutes for Social Housing. The planning process was to become more centralized and its criteria more uniform, whereas the operational phase was to be decentralized. At the centre, the Interministerial Committees for Economic Planning and for Dwelling Construction were to lay down over-all criteria for building plans and the allocation of funds such as, for instance, the assignment of earmarked shares of available finance to immigrant housing, to people living in barracks, to students' hostels, and, more generally, to the South. The regions were to assume direct responsibility for the preparation and execution of building plans within the framework of over-all regional planning. They were also to have a say in the communal town plans and expropriation programmes and in the distribution of funds. The direct executors of building programmes would be the Autonomous Institutes of Social Housing but the regions could also have recourse to public corporations.

There are three forms of financial incentive for house-building: public subsidies, fiscal and credit incentives, and a new kind of contractual arrangement intended to orient private investment towards social housing and to control rents and prices for dwellings. This last involves commitments by building firms as to the type of houses to be built, the prices to be charged, and the categories to whom they are to be supplied.

A revolving fund of 150 billion lire has been foreseen to pay for the expropriations and another fund of 300 billion lire is intended for acquisition and urbanization of other areas. In the past, 50 per cent of investment in housing has been financed directly by private investors, about 43 per cent by various credit institutions, insurance companies, and building societies, and some 7 per cent by the public sector. The reform provides for a change in the sources of finance. Public and subsidized housing is to account for 25 per cent of the total and the private sector for 75 per cent. The very large increase in the contribution of public financing to dwelling construction will require increases in public bond issues, and the problem therefore arises of how to attract a part of the private savings formerly channelled directly to highly profitable investment in housing into the purchase of securities.

The provisions of the housing reform constitute in theory a considerable improvement on previous arrangements. In practice, however, it soon turned out that these were half-way solutions. In the private sector, the uncertainties connected with expropriation and, more generally, with the concrete repercussions of the reform checked the previous substantial direct flow of private investment funds to house-building. In the public sector, the many gaps left by the reform in the institutional and financial machinery at the regional and communal level are preventing its speedy implementation. The transfer of many tasks in planning and executing social housing programmes to the regions has not been accompanied, so far, by the setting up of an appropriate regional administration; and this has delayed the preparation and approval of town-planning mechanisms, upon which the implementation of other elements of the reform depend. Financial problems have also been tackled only in part. No answer to the question how to provide public funds on the scale required by the reform has been offered; the funds so far available to the central authorities are limited, and even these have not yet been allocated because of lack of co-ordination of legislative with administrative provisions.

The delays have permitted the crystallization of a great deal of opposition to the reform, some of it fomented by political interests and used for electoral purposes. Expropriation was obviously not a popular measure among land-owners near urban centres, and among real-estate speculators and building firms there were also violent protests. Even many of the intended future beneficiaries of the reform joined the ranks of the opposition, largely because a new formula for leasehold (as well as freehold) ownership, hitherto unknown in Italy, for socially provided or promoted housing ran counter to a deep-seated preference for ownership.

The housing reform has thus so far resulted in a deadlock. It has become another issue for political controversy and an obstacle, rather than a stimulus, to the revival of dwelling construction in general and the supply of low-cost housing in particular.

(ii) THE HEALTH REFORM

The existing level and quality of health services and the prolonged discussions on the objectives and instruments of a health-service reform provide another example of the deficiencies of social institutions in Italy, of the inertia of public administration, and of political pressures by various interest groups.

Some quantitative and qualitative indications help to illustrate the problems which have to be faced: the infant mortality rate in Italy is 30·9 per thousand, much higher still in the South, and Italy has descended in this respect from the thirteenth to the eighteenth place among European countries in recent years. Italy also has an exceptionally high (and rising) rate of accidents and sickness in factories. In 1971 there were 1,640,000 accidents at work, of which 5,000 were fatal. Special health services for old people are practically non-existent; and the general health service, covering some 50 million persons, concentrates on diagnosis and cure and pays little attention to preventive treatment.

The First Economic Plan for 1966–70 set an investment target for the improvement of health services. Only 35 per cent of this target was achieved and the shortfall was much larger in the South. The building of new hospitals suffered from the general defects in the system of preparing, financing, and executing investment projects common to all public investment programmes. Conditions for patients and personnel have deteriorated considerably and have been one of the causes of repeated strikes of doctors, nurses, and other hospital staff.

The indicator of hospital beds per thousand inhabitants is not very meaningful in Italian conditions, except to show up regional differences. The problem of overcrowding in hospitals is more a reflection of the lack of subsidiary services which could make a first diagnosis and act as filter to hospital admission. Hence hospitals are called upon to admit as patients people who ought to be dealt with by out-patients departments, clinics, or first-aid stations. Neither can one speak of an over-all shortage of doctors but rather of their uneven distribution and undue concentration in the large urban centres.

As also in other fields of social consumption and investment, the health system is rendered cumbersome and costly through the multiplicity of its institutions. Their expenditure has risen by over 80 per cent from 1965 to 1970 whereas ordinary receipts increased by only 61 per cent, and their annual deficit has risen four-fold. According to the Minister of Health, contributions to health insurance absorbed a higher share of wages than in any other Common Market country, whereas the services rendered are quantitatively and qualitatively the worst.

Among the reasons for the rapid rise in expenditure by health-insurance institutions was the fact that free supply stimulated demand and resulted in an excessive use of pharmaceutical and hospital services. But while payments for pharmaceuticals have expanded most rapidly in the past, rising hospital costs have been the main cause of the acceleration of expenditures more recently. Apart from higher wages and salaries for hospital personnel and other increases in running costs, the basis for calculating the sums to be allocated to individual hospitals by the health-insurance institutions has discouraged efficiency and cost-reduction. They are based on the bed occupancy rate in the preceding year; and this tends to discourage the limitation of the hospitalization period to the real need of the patient. In fact, the average duration of hospitalization in Italy is among the longest in the world, which does *not* imply that the chronic sick are a higher proportion of the hospital population than in other countries.

Thus the lack of a suitable diversity of health services, and of sufficient attention to standards of public hygiene and sanitation, has caused a progressive increase in recourse to existing services and a deterioration of their quality. The Second Economic Plan for 1971–75 stressed not only the need for improvement, but also the need to replace the existing system of insurance against sickness by a system guaranteeing the full right to the protection of health, which makes prevention a major objective.

The health reform has not yet taken any precise shape; but there seems to be general agreement on some basic principles. One is the establishment of a National Health Service and the abolition of all existing health-insurance institutions, with the financing of the new system to be partly shifted to the budget and away from social security contributions. The organization of the health service is to be on three levels. General directives on criteria and standards are to be issued by Central organs—the Minister of Health and a National Health Council composed of experts, administrators, and operators; and finance is to be allocated to the regions through the Ministry's budget. The regions are to plan and supervise the system, and under their directives, Local Health Units (catering for groups from 30,000 to 100,000 persons) are to implement the reform and run the new system. The hope is to increase efficiency, avoid waste, and ensure democratic control.

As has already been seen in connection with the housing reform, there is a general tendency to transfer tasks in the social field to the regional authorities. However, while some executive powers have been handed over to the regions, the necessary institutions for the exercise of their powers have not yet been created and their sphere for legislative action has not yet been clearly defined. In these circumstances, old institutional arrangements continued to operate in the customary setting of arbitrary decisions and political pull.

No precise plan has so far been formulated for the financing of the health reform. In the Second Economic Plan it was estimated that expenditure on health would rise from 3·1 billion lire in 1971 to 4·9 billion in 1975, and to this 1·8 billion need for new finance must be added the existing deficit of the health service institutions, which amounted to some 1·4 billion lire in 1971. A figure of one billion lire for financing by the budget out of taxation has frequently been mentioned; part of the necessary funds will continue to be provided by social security contributions; and it is intended to cut costs through closer control over the production and distribution of pharmaceuticals, improvement of the efficiency of hospital services and their method of financing, and some disciplining of the medical profession so that, while adequate remuneration and continuous improvement of professional qualification are guaranteed, exploitation of a monopoly position is prevented.

The institutional and financing problems are admittedly difficult and will take time to solve. But, once again, as is the usual experience in conditions of uncertainty and hesitation, opposition has become vociferous both from political parties and their factions and from vested interests such as the existing health service institutions, private hospitals, members of the medical profession, and the pharmaceutical industries; and the political courage to counter or side-step such opposition so far has been lacking in the originators of this reform project, as of many others.

(iii) THE REFORM OF THE PUBLIC ADMINISTRATION

The reform of the public administration is a basic condition upon which all other reforms, including the speeding up of public investment projects, largely depend. A Ministry of Bureaucratic Reform has been set up for this purpose but, so far, little if any progress has been made in improving the functioning of the government machinery.

The public administration is established on lines decided upon more than a century ago. While its tasks have been both growing and becoming increasingly complex, the Government apparatus has remained rigid, monolithic, authoritarian, and hierarchic. The public administration 'knows only functions, not objectives; only rules, not alternatives; only rigid procedures, not choices'.[2]

Economic policy-making is split between three Ministries—the Treasury, the Ministry of the Budget and Economic Planning, and the Ministry of Finance; and more specific economic functions are assigned to the Ministries of State Participations, the South, and Industry. Economic planning has not been entrusted to an independent outside body (as in France) but forms part of the Ministry of the Budget. The new Centro-Sinistra Government formed in July 1973, has maintained the division of Ministries but at least the appointment as Ministers of three experienced economic experts with a certain convergency of views may soften the adverse effect of a division of powers.

The central administration is organized on a sectoral basis rather than being geared to specific objectives and functions; and this tends to 'place Ministries in direct contact with corporative interests, thus linking their choices to the intensity of pressures from interest groups rather than to the priorities dictated by planning objectives'.[3] On the other hand, they remain out of touch with citizens' problems and preferences and are reluctant to create institutions which would permit a wider democratic participation in Government. The decision-making process of the Government machine is slowed down excessively by detailed legislation even on minor issues, and by a multiplicity of controls, in particular over allocations of public funds, which go through many administrative phases of approval, verification, and checking. And 'the more numerous the controls, the greater the power of the bureaucracy and the smaller its responsibility.'[4]

Instead of adapting the basic machinery, the response of the public authorities to the challenge of the growing and novel tasks of government in an industrial society took the form of a proliferation of tens of thousands of public agencies, the creation of extra-budgetary funds and the growth of a 'parallel bureaucracy'. New agencies were set up in an *ad hoc* manner, when and where the need arose, and without any precise directives, delimitation of functions, or provision for effective central control. One result was an enormous expansion of public employment—by 58 per cent from 1951 to 1971 while employment in industry increased by 40 per cent and total employment declined. The share of public employees in total employment rose from 5·3 per cent to over 9 per cent; and in the South alone the increase was from 5·8 to 10·4 per cent, even though the seat of central government is outside the region.

The characteristics of the public administration make co-ordinated and coherent action to achieve policy objectives almost impossible. They help to explain the extraordinarily slow workings of the government machinery, the power of individual pressure groups, the frequently arbitrary and contradictory decisions and the pervasive resistance to change. One of the most flagrant manifestations of these defects has been the accumulation of unspent appropriations for public expenditure. 'If there is a field which testifies to the difficulty political forces encounter in overcoming bureaucratic resistance and technocratic and administrative prevarications, it is in that of the institutional reform of the budget.'[5]

Proposals for a reform of the public administration have been put forward in 'Projections to 1980', an official document on the basis of which the plan for 1971–5 was drawn up. They advocate a division of tasks between the central administrations and decentralized functional departments. The former would be responsible for economic planning in general, the clear definition of policy objectives, the elaboration of directives and financial control; the latter would be entrusted with the detailed formulation and execution of policy and projects, and would dispose of sufficient financial autonomy and organizational flexibility to speed up operational procedures. By concentrating operational activities in the functional administrations, the 'uncertain sphere of agencies of varying nature and dimension in which sinecures prosper and "sub-government activities" abound' would be eliminated.[6] Decentralization should, at the same time, lead to a democratization of public management, for instance through wider participation of citizens' representatives in the administration of social services and through access to information from which they have been barred in the past. More generally, trade unions and the regions should take an active part at all stages of the decision-making process.

So far, opposition to changes which would threaten positions of power and privilege in the higher echelons, and the security of employment at the lower levels, has come from the bureaucracy itself; and the reform of the public administration has remained a dead letter. A minor provision for anticipated retirement, aiming to reduce the numbers in public employment, has had rather paradoxical results. Strong incentives have recently been granted for early retirement from high-level civil service jobs, in the form of promotions to higher grades of those willing to retire and extension of their recorded length of service. Thus they receive pensions based on an inflated terminal salary and severance pay based on a fictitious number of years of employment. Such attractive conditions induced a large number of officials to retire; and incidentally over 60 per cent of the senior officials of the Ministry of Finance retired just at the time when the second part of the tax reform was to be finalized. But since the inducements were offered non-selectively, it was on the whole the more efficient and the younger of the top civil servants who chose to resign, since they could count on finding interesting alternative employment, perhaps even in other branches of the public sector. This costly 'reform' involved another diversion of public expenditure from much-needed investment to current outlays and the loss of some of the best elements in the public administration, leaving some gaps which could be difficult to fill effectively, at least in the short run.

A major step towards a genuine reform of the public administration might well have been taken, however, with the transfer of a number of functions to the regions. The granting of regional autonomy and the principle of an administrative decentralization had already been stipulated by the Constitution of 1947; and the Constitution also listed the fields in which the regions were to exercise their administrative and legislative authority. Among these are regional town-planning, local transport, health and hospital services, roads and public works of regional interest, tourism, handicrafts, agriculture and forestry and, more recently, environmental problems. But it was only in the spring of 1971 that the transfer of functions and of part of the personnel from the central authorities to the regions at last took place.

The regional reform may turn out to be a decisive opportunity for transforming the public administration in the direction of greater flexibility, accelerated procedures, more concern with local interests and more democratic participation in economic and social policy decisions. On the other hand, it also involves the dangers that the regional authorities may reproduce the defects of the central administration at their own level, that there may be duplication of tasks, a further swelling of public offices and the creation of a new regional political class bargaining for mutual concessions and benefits and the emergence of new pressure groups. The transfer of powers has been slow and there is strong resistance to it, both from the centre and from the communal authorities as also from the civil servants who are to be transferred. It is thus too early to say whether positive or negative results will predominate.

So far, the defects in the structure of the central administrations constitute, of themselves, a major obstacle to the successful functioning of regional institutions. The effective transfer of functions to the regions requires that the central administration should limit its actions to the issue of directives and co-ordination and not interfere with detailed administration and operational decisions. As it is, the state continues to superimpose itself on, and to duplicate the functions of, the regional authorities in fields which have formally been assigned to the latter; and the sectoral organization of the government machinery itself hampers the formulation and execution of co-ordinated and integrated development programmes in the regions.

Moreover, the division of legislative powers has not been sufficiently clearly specified. The Constitution provided for legislative autonomy in the fields over which the regions have been given authority. On the other hand, the central authorities must, within a given time-limit, vote framework laws specifying the basic principles according to which the regions can legislate. If these laws have not been voted when the time-limit expires, regional councils acquire freedom of legislation. Such stipulations can give rise to recurrent conflict, and one experience illustrates the problems which may arise: when some regions voted the finance required to accelerate construction of low-cost housing, in anticipation of the provision of central finance, the central authorities objected and the matter had to be brought before the Constitutional Court. Meanwhile Parliament continued to legislate on innumerable minor questions which should fall within regional jurisdiction.

Other obstacles to the exercise of regional functions are the limited resources of the Fund for Regional Development and the fact that its allocation is linked to sectoral purposes and not to more comprehensive development projects; and the structure of the budget, based on appropriations for administrative Departments and not on an allocation of planned expenditures to priority objectives and projects, affects regional as well as national development and prevents the co-ordination of regional with national expenditure plans.

Finally, there is a close mutual interdependence between an efficient and purposeful functioning of the central and regional public administration and effective economic planning. Economic planning has been hampered in Italy by an inefficient, incoherent, and slow-working public administration. Conversely, the co-ordination of central and regional administrative activities to achieve over-all economic and social aims depends on the clear formulation of objectives, within the framework of a coherent longer-term plan taking account of both regional and national needs, and on success in mobilizing wide popular consensus and support.

CHAPTER 9

ECONOMIC PLANNING

THE introduction of 'economic planning' as a means of achieving a structural transformation of the Italian economy has been under discussion for many years. The first official planning document which presented a reasoned argument on objectives, and the resources required to attain them, was the Vanoni Plan for the development of employment and income in Italy in the decade 1955–64. It gave rise to a great deal of discussion but was not followed by concrete action, partly because it was widely believed at the time that the rapid expansion under way would spontaneously reduce structural imbalances. In 1962 an 'Additional Note' to the Annual Report of the Ministry of the Budget stated that sectoral and regional problems and the social backwardness of the country could not be expected to be corrected through the operation of market forces alone and that the introduction of planning methods and instruments was needed. These ideas were further developed in a report by Professor P. Saraceno, the Vice-President of a previously established National Commission for Economic Planning, which was presented in 1963; and the first National Economic Programme for the period 1966–70, inspired by the 'Note' and the Saraceno Report, was approved by the Council of Ministers in January 1965. It was passed by Parliament only in July 1967, when a part of the planning period had already elapsed.

The objectives of this plan were:

1. Full employment of the labour force.
2. Elimination of the gap between the South and the rest of the country.
3. A progressive equalization of labour income in agriculture and in non-agricultural activities.
4. A redistribution of resources in favour of such collective needs as schools, housing, health, social security, pro-

fessional training, transport, urban development, soil conservation, and scientific research.

The over-all annual growth rate, within which these objectives were to be attained, was set at 5 per cent, and quantitative targets were established for the major economic variables.

A confrontation of the targets or forecasts of the First National Economic Programme with the results achieved reflects both the difficulties encountered through the inadequacy of institutions and instruments for plan implementation and the deterioration of economic conditions in recent years. It also helps to indicate the directions in which subsequent planning efforts were to be concentrated.

The quantitative comparison of targets and realizations shows, in the first place, that the potential annual growth rate of GNP had been greatly underestimated by the planners. The actual growth rate reached nearly 6 per cent, instead of the forecast 5 per cent, and productivity increased at an annual rate of 6·2 per cent compared with the forecast 4·2 per cent. The employment objective of the Plan was an increase of 800,000; instead there was a decline by 172,000. The development of the labour force, and the large increase in the non-active population, have already been analysed in Chapter 5.

A larger balance-of-payments surplus, on goods and services account, absorbed two-thirds of the additional GNP generated over the whole five-year period while productive and public social investment fell short of the target, the latter very substantially. The only categories of domestic expenditure which surpassed the forecasts for the five years were investment in housing and private consumption. The former was entirely due to the supply by the private sector of high-cost or medium-cost dwellings, while social provision of housing for the lower-income groups remained wholly inadequate. Public consumption expenditure on education and health attained 93·6 per cent of the five-year target level, public social investment reached only 57·7 per cent of the target.

TABLE 16

Economic Plan 1966–70,
five-year totals, targets and realizations
(Thousand billion lire at 1963 prices)

	Targets		*Realization*	
	lire	% of total resources	lire	% of total resources
Supply:				
GNP	192·6	99·7	200·0	102·8
Net imports	+0·5	+0·3	−5·5	−2·8
Total	193·1	100·0	194·5	100·0
Use:				
Productive investment	22·6	11·7	22·3	11·0
Agriculture	4·3	2·2	3·1	1·6
Industry	18·3	9·5	18·4	9·4
Changes in stocks	2·0	1·0	1·1	1·0
Social expenditure	43·4	22·5	42·5	21·9
Private (Housing)[1]	7·1	3·7	11·6	5·9
Public consumption	25·1	13·0	24·5	12·6
Public social investment[1]	11·2	5·9	6·4	3·3
Private consumption	125·1	65·0	128·8	65·2

1. The division of total social investment into these two categories is derived from the O.E.C.D., *Economic Surveys, Italy* (1972).

Source: Segretario Generale della Programmazione Economica, Appendix to 'Rapporto sull, Esperienza di Programmazione' (1973).

The figures in Table 17 indicate that the most substantial short-falls in social public investment occurred in those sectors which most directly serve collective needs. The sectors for which results considerably exceeded plan targets were those which responded to impulses from private and individual demand where 'public intervention is limited to supplying infra-structures on which individual production or consumption is based'.[1]

The plan foresaw nominal *per capita* income from employment increasing at about the same rate as productivity; and, assuming price stability, this was to ensure that nominal and real income increases moved in step, that savings were adequate and that the return on capital would be such as not to discourage investment. In fact, price stability was not

TABLE 17

Economic Plan 1966–70,
public social investment, five-year totals, targets and realizations
(Billion lire at 1963 prices)

	Target	Realization	Realization as percentage of target
Education	960	347	36·1
Public Housing	2,380	700	29·4
Health	360	123	34·2
Transport	4,125	3,020	73·2
of which:			
Urban transport	235	80	34·0
Airports and civil aviation	95	295	310·5
Telecommunications	715	925	129·4
Public works	2,270	1,313	57·8
Total	11,140	6,428	57·7

Source: as for Table 16.

achieved and the money remuneration of factors of production increased faster than productivity, which itself rose more rapidly than forecast. The total volume of gross savings exceeded the Plan figure and reached 24 per cent of GNP instead of the foreseen 22·3 per cent; but the volume of domestic investment was lower than forecast and absorbed 82 per cent of gross savings against the 94 per cent foreseen, the difference being reflected in the balance-of-payments surplus.

One Plan target was to raise agricultural *per capita* income from 47 per cent to 52 per cent of the level of non-agricultural income; and this was surpassed in money terms. But the improvement in the distribution of money income was largely absorbed by an unfavourable development of relative prices. Moreover, agricultural employment was reduced at twice the rate anticipated by the Plan and the agricultural development pattern differed fundamentally from the intended shift of output away from labour-extensive crops to meat, fruit and vegetable production.

The target for narrowing the gap between the South and the national average was to reduce the difference between value added per man in the South and in the country as a whole from 22 per cent to 15–16 per cent. In reality the gap increased to 24 per cent. The outflow from agriculture in the South was 438,000 workers instead of the forecast 350,000, while the increase of employment in non-agricultural activities was 294,000 instead of 590,000. As a result the South accounted for the whole of the short-fall by 300,000 on the planned increase in non-agricultural employment, but for only 22 per cent of the 100 per cent increase in the outflow from agriculture in the whole of Italy.

The essential features of the draft for the Second National Economic Programme for the period 1971–5 were accepted by the Interministerial Committee on Economic Planning—once again with some delay—in July 1972; and a revised plan for the period 1973–7 is to be prepared on that basis. The changes in the Second Plan are derived from the lessons learnt from the First Plan and from a prior document on 'Projections to 1980' which provides a longer-term horizon.

The Plan itself now consists of three parts. The first is a general five-year development plan to serve as a frame of reference. It contains the usual general objectives translated into quantitative targets, hypotheses on the behaviour of various exogenous variables over which the central authorities have no control, and indications on the magnitude of instrument variables. The objectives do not differ in substance from those of the first programme—full employment, the elimination of regional gaps, and the improvement of the social, environmental, and cultural framework of the economy. The success of the Plan will be seen not so much in a precise achievement of quantitative targets but in whether the economy can be oriented in the directions indicated by them. The planning framework should serve to co-ordinate discussion and action by the central government, the regions, and also enterprises and trade unions; and consultations, in the phases both of elaboration and implementation, are to form part of the planning process.

The second part of the Plan consists of 'programme actions', divided into two major groups:

1. Those which serve to modernize and strengthen infrastructures on which the social and economic life of a modern country is based; these require institutional reforms and a larger contribution of public expenditure to balanced economic development.
2. Those which serve to bring about a structural transformation and modernization of the productive system, in the direction of a transformation and rationalization of traditional productive activities—mainly agriculture, the development of new activities, and the location of new plants in the light of regional planning objectives.

The third part of the Plan consists of Annual Plans which are to provide flexibility for a continuing adjustment to changes in the initial hypotheses and a continuing check on the coherence of short-term developments, economic policies, and medium-term objectives; they are also to ensure consistency of programme actions with the general plan and to provide the basis for annual financing plans.

Generally, the new features of the Plan are insistence on a clearly specified operational content, through the introduction of 'programme projects', and the provision of a 'framework for co-ordinating a continuous flow of decisions rather than an immutable set of targets set up once and for all'.[2]

There is no point in presenting the quantitative forecasts of expenditure, output, and employment in detail. These have by now become obsolete, and the presentation and adoption of the revised plan for 1973–7 has been postponed for the time being. But some of the features of the plan serve to indicate its main directions. Taking account of the 1971 recession, GNP growth was to slow down during the plan period, to rates below those achieved in the 1960s, but to accelerate substantially by the end of the 1970s. A shift in the composition of domestic demand was intended both for the plan period and the 1970s as a whole, with private consumption giving way to a higher rate of expansion of productive investment but above all to social expenditure. For the balance of payments on current account a reduction of the surplus was forecast in the longer run, involving a corresponding reduction of capital outflows, the latter to take the form of investment in, and direct aid to, developing countries rather than of portfolio investment in industrial countries.

The decline in total employment was to turn into an increase during the latter part of the plan period; and a strong expansion of demand, resulting from 'programme actions' in productive sectors and from social expenditure, was expected to increase activity rates. The investments foreseen aimed to raise employment by 200,000. This is an ambitious target in that it includes the absorption both of precarious employment in the South and in the tertiary sector in general and of a continuing, although slower, outflow from agriculture. Since large productivity advances are required to maintain Italy's competitive position and to permit further wage increases, an increase of employment sufficient to absorb labour released from agriculture and from precarious employment requires a high rate of increase of the demand for labour in other sectors. Special efforts are needed to expand activities with a high labour-intensity while at the same time supporting the growth of technologically advanced sectors.

The development policies for the South are expected to encounter greater difficulties. The renewed over-all expansion tends to favour investment in existing enterprises in the North, and the shortage of infra-structures and social services in the North competes with the South for claims on public funds. The measures intended to overcome these obstacles have been outlined in Chapter 6. But, in addition, all 'programme actions' of the Plan are to be carefully examined in the light of their direct and indirect effects on the economy of the South.

The lessons to be drawn from the planning experience have been summarized in a document, 'Rapporto sull'Esperienza di Programmazione' (Report on the Experience of Planning), by the Secretary of Planning, published in February 1973. He reaffirms his conviction that only a policy of planning and reform can solve the problems of the Italian economy and stresses the need to clarify the reasons which have so far prevented planning from playing the role assigned to it by its promoters.

The Italian planning experience so far is generally considered to have been a partial failure. In the first place, the law which approved the first programme did not provide for concrete action but limited itself to a declaration that the Government was authorized to take appropriate steps; and the Government itself had discussed and approved the Plan with little conviction and had placed little emphasis on implementation or the transmission of effective directives to the various decision-centres. Special planning institutions were set up; but both their funds and the staff at their disposal were inadequate for the functions they were supposed to fulfil, and they had to operate within a wider institutional framework which made it virtually impossible to translate proposed actions into reality. As has been stressed before, the public administration is ineffectual in carrying out the ordinary tasks of economic management, let alone those of ambitious economic planning; budgetary instruments are ill-adapted to deliberate longer-term action and no provisions have so far been made for formulating longer-term budgets coinciding with the plan period. While the Plan indicated certain reforms required to adapt existing institutions, many of the proposed reforms have been unduly delayed or only partially enacted; and those which have been implemented have often failed to operate as intended. Little support for or confidence in, planning methods was shown by the organized social groups; and the enterprise sector in particular often saw in planning a 'socialist' threat.

The idea of planning has, in fact, become widely discredited. Yet the introduction of planning concepts and visions into political discussion and policy statements has produced some important modifications in attitudes and institutions. It has at least produced a greater awareness of the need for rational criteria and related objectives, to render policy-making less empirical and more systematic; and it has stimulated economic and statistical research and improved knowledge of how the economic system operates. Closer contacts have been gradually established between the Government, enterprises, and trade unions, and between the central and regional authorities. There is now a widespread consciousness of the urgency of reforms and a greater pressure to bring them about.

The documents of the Second Plan reflect progress made in rendering planning methods more sophisticated and planning procedures more realistic, flexible, and operational, at least in principle. But, in the last resort, the success or failure of the new planning strategy must depend on a rapid transformation of public institutions and a more effective use of policy instruments. A positive factor is the conviction of the new Government that the seriousness of the present economic and social situation does not permit any further hesitation and delay. Another failure would risk permanently destroying confidence in the political will to remove structural disequilibria, and would start off, once again, the vicious circle of wage claims and social unrest, inflationary pressures and policies of restraint, which, in turn, threaten to check expansion and the revival of productive investment and to compromise the longer-term aim of balanced economic development.

CHAPTER 10

CONCLUDING REMARKS

THREE more months were put at my disposal after the completion of the preceding chapters to give a brief description of recent economic developments and policy decisions and to attempt an assessment of the prospects of the Italian economy. This chapter is therefore based on information available at the end of December 1973; but of course it can still not take adequate account of the impact of the oil crisis on output, employment, the rate of inflation and the balance of payments.

(i) ECONOMIC DEVELOPMENTS IN 1973

The renewed economic expansion which had begun in the latter part of 1972 after some three years of recession was interrupted by labour conflicts in the early part of 1973. It was resumed in the second quarter and has since gathered momentum. For the whole of 1973, real GNP growth has been estimated at 5 per cent, compared with rates of expansion of 1·6 and 3·2 per cent in 1971 and 1972.

The acceleration of economic growth was supported by the expansionary impact of the budget and by reflationary monetary policies and was at first led entirely by domestic expenditures. Private consumption speeded up after two years of moderate growth. It was boosted by the substantial concessions of the last wage-round (20 to 30 per cent), by automatic wage adjustments to the cost of living which were only partially absorbed by price increases, and by higher transfer payments. Residential construction revived after a three-year recession and productive investment also recovered in response to rising final demand, higher profits, and better business prospects. Investment in 1973 is expected to add some 5 to 6 per cent to productive capacities.

The volume of exports, on the other hand, rose at an exceptionally low rate. The short-fall of industrial production due to strikes in the first quarter of the year prevented exporters from benefiting from buoyant world demand; but deliveries picked up again in the second quarter and accelerated subsequently.

On the supply side, industrial production speeded up after the first quarter, and almost all sectors of industrial activity participated in the upswing. A rapid rise in the volume of imports, due in part to speculative stock-building, added to the resources available for matching supply to rising demand.

The average degree of capacity utilization in industry exceeded that of 1971 and 1972 but has not yet attained 1969 and 1970 levels. Although previous peak rates may be difficult to reach in future, as a consequence of the changes in rules on overtime and shift work conceded to trade union demands, capacity limits are not expected to check further industrial expansion in the short run. The higher demand for labour has reduced unemployment (mainly of male workers), under-employment, and the number of first-job seekers. But it has failed to increase the labour supply through re-entries into the labour market from the reservoir of the non-active population. The structural factors which account for this phenomenon, and explain the co-existence of labour shortages with a persistent under-utilization of the labour potential, have been analysed in Chapter 5.

The acceleration of demand and output was, nevertheless, accompanied by several external and domestic strains. First, the exchange rate of the lira had depreciated on average by 20 per cent below its January level by June, a tendency which was reinforced by and contributed to domestic inflation. Second, for both internal and external reasons, consumer and wholesale prices of manufactures rose in the first nine months of the year at annual rates of 12 and 18 per cent respectively, rates unprecedented in Italy and exceeding also those of nearly all industrial countries (consumer prices in Japan and wholesale prices in the United States rose faster). Third, the current account of the balance of payments recorded a large deficit, the first since 1963. Exports had risen in value much more slowly than imports (by some 15 as against 40 per cent) although the depreciation of the lira made it possible to adjust prices to higher costs without endangering the competitive position of Italian export commodities. The abnormal increase in the value of imports was due above all to the sharp rise in unit values, about one-half accounted for by the depreciation of the lira and the rest by an unprecedented increase in world prices. There was a sharp fall in net receipts from tourism and from emigrants' remittances, which reflected disguised capital exports. The capital account proper registered a surplus, thanks largely to compensatory borrowing abroad and to measures taken to check speculative capital exports; and both these factors and the upturn of exports during the year contributed towards strengthening the lira in August and stabilizing it in October at an average rate of depreciation since the beginning-of-the-year level of some 15 per cent. Finally, the budget deficit increased at a high and accelerating rate.

(ii) THE SHORT-TERM EMERGENCY PROGRAMME

The Centro-Sinistra coalition Government took over in July 1973 in an atmosphere of crisis and deep concern. Terms such as the 'hundred days programme' and 'the last beach' were intended to provide a psychological shock, to convey the seriousness of the situation and the need for immediate and energetic action against inflation. In fact, policy decisions were taken and legislation was passed at an unprecedented speed, and the Troika of economic Ministers together with the Governor of the Bank of Italy proceeded to adopt remedial measures with a new determination, coherence, and unity.

The policy programme for a first phase which lasted until the end of October consisted of four sets of measures: a price freeze, new provisions to prevent speculative capital exports (which have been described in Chapter 4), selective credit controls, and budget austerity.

The control of prices

To slow down price increases the following measures were taken on 25 July: first, to protect the real incomes of the working population and to reduce automatic wage adjustments, the prices of 21 mass-consumption goods were blocked; secondly, rents paid by lower income groups were frozen; thirdly, enterprises with a turnover of more than 5 billion lira in the first half of 1973 had to deposit with the Interministerial Committee on Prices (CIP) price lists of the goods they distributed or produced. Future variations of both the consumer-goods prices and the prices charged by the large enterprises became subject to authorization, on the basis of requests to be supported by evidence on cost variations and changes in market conditions.

On the whole, the first phase of the freeze of consumer-goods prices was considered a success. A highly tentative estimate by ISCO suggests that, together with already previously controlled and 'administered' prices, and the effect on free prices of the freeze of the price lists of large enterprises, prices affecting more than one-half of household expenditure were controlled. In fact, the rate of increase of consumer prices slowed down from a monthly average of 1·1 per cent in the first half of 1973 to 0·6 per cent in July and August. And the automatic cost-of-living adjustment of wages was substantially lower than in the earlier part of the year. But this result cannot be wholly attributed to the measures taken. Some uncontrolled prices also rose less rapidly than in the recent past, partly in response to increases in supply, of food in particular, and partly because of a psychological reaction to the price freeze.

The rate of increase of wholesale prices also slowed down to 1·2 per cent in August, or about half the rate of preceding months. Prices of products produced or traded by smaller enterprises and of imported goods played roles varying from product to product, as there are very wide differences both between major sectors and within manufacturing in the degree of concentration.

For the second phase of price control, which started on 1 November, it was decided to continue the price freeze for mass-consumption goods until after Christmas. For these goods, price increases may be conceded on the basis of higher raw-material costs only; and, on these grounds, the first authorization for an increase has been granted for an Italian staple food—pasta. For the prices charged by the large enterprises the rigid control has been replaced by a selective and more flexible policy. This is to permit adjustments to cost changes but, according to official statements, an attempt will be made to 'avoid sudden variations excessively concentrated in time'. The controls must remain severe because it is feared that a renewed upward drift of prices might 'strengthen economic and social tensions, provoke uncontrollable wage demands and hence threaten the consolidation of the upturn of production and the revival of investment'.

As in other countries where a temporary price freeze has been tried out, the passage from phase one to phase two will be the crucial test of price-control policies. It has generally been found that, although a temporary price freeze can help to break the price–wage spiral, it cannot be sustained for long without raising serious problems of enforcement, of distortion of economic structures, and of negative effects on efficiency. Further, a combination of a strong collective discipline with a highly efficient administrative machinery is required—conditions which can hardly be said to be met in Italy. In particular, the passing from an automatic mechanism of price control to an efficient selective and flexible one requires institutions equipped to collect, and to use appropriately, a great deal of information on the highly divergent situations of different industrial branches and enterprises. Information is required not only on cost factors but also on the market structures in which enterprises operate and on other variables. Moreover, raw-material price increases are expected to continue and cost increases in some sectors had not yet been passed on to prices before the freeze. The rise of oil prices following the Middle Eastern crisis constitutes another serious threat to price-stabilization policies.

Whatever the success of the short-term measures, the trade union confederations insist that the steps taken or contemplated so far tackle only the manifestations of inflation, not its root causes. They point out, for instance, that excessively high rents for low income groups stemmed from the failure in the past to provide publicly supported social housing, that high food prices were in part the outcome of erroneous agricultural policies, and that retail prices are excessively burdened by high distribution costs.

Selective credit control

The monetary authorities were faced with the complex task of trying to interrupt the inflationary spiral without checking investment; to limit credit expansion for speculative purposes (capital exports and stockbuilding which affect the balance of payments and prices) without restricting finance for productive investment and in particular without hitting small and medium-sized firms; to stabilize long-term interest rates while permitting short-term rates to adjust to levels prevailing in other financial markets; and to finance the Treasury deficit in a way which would limit its inflationary impact.

In the first half of 1973, banks had liquidated part of their security portfolios to meet the rising demand for credit. This created difficulties in placing new issues with the banking sector for the special credit institutions (which finance medium and long-term investments), the public corporations, and private companies.

A series of selective measures was adopted between June and October 1973. To transfer resources from the money to the capital market and stabilize long-term interest rates, the banks were compelled to purchase securities for not less than 6 per cent of the deposits they held at the end of 1972. The special credit institutions were requested to issue securities so as to increase their investment-financing resources. The former measure implied a limitation of the expansion of short-term credit, which was considered desirable so as to adjust short-term interest rates to those prevailing in other financial centres.

To protect small and medium-sized enterprises from the restrictive impact of these measures, the increase of larger bank loans was limited to 12 per cent, though loans for pre-financing were exempt from this rule. But the limit was applied also to smaller loans to wholesale and retail trade and some other categories, which might be borrowing largely for speculative purposes.

Short-term interest rates rose; and official interest rates were raised in line with market rates at home and abroad.

To finance part of the cash requirements of the Treasury, an issue of Treasury bonds for an amount of 1,300 billion lire, with a duration of 6 months and at a competitive interest rate of 9·5 per cent, was authorized. The issue was at first entirely subscribed by the central bank but was subsequently offered to the commercial banks so as to avoid an excessive increase in the monetary base.

It is too early as yet to assess the impact of these measures, in particular whether the ultimate impact on productive investment will be restrictive and whether small and medium-sized firms will in fact be protected from the credit squeeze. So far, credit restraint seems to have had no overall impact on investment. This can be explained by the fact that profits had begun to rise in the latter part of 1972 and that these were used at first for accumulating financial assets and raw material stocks rather than for financing new investments. When capital expenditure began to expand subsequently, it could be financed by a liquidation of these assets rather than through recourse to new credit. But this alternative source of finance must eventually dry up. Smaller enterprises will be affected by the higher cost of short-term credit, to the extent that they rely on a renewal of short-term credit lines for investment finance. Moreover, credit standing rather than the purpose of the intended investment is the criterion usually applied by banks, and large borrowers tend to be preferred when credit is tight. Among speculative transactions, capital exports have been reduced by these measures as well as by the more direct checks on capital outflows.

Budget austerity

A major concern of the authorities is the inflationary impact of the general-government budget deficit, which has been growing by leaps and bounds since 1970. The recent rise has been due to the under-utilization of resources caused by the recession, which necessitated substantial increases in transfer payments and the absorption into public employment of part of the redundant labour force. But the spreading to the public sector of large industrial wage increases granted in the wage-rounds of 1970 and 1973 also played a role. In 1973, the low receipts from V.A.T. in the first year after its introduction were another factor; and a short-fall of direct tax revenue is expected in 1974, the first year in which the reform of direct taxation begins to function. But there have also been structural causes for the growing deficit. Italy's tax ratio is exceptionally low by international standards, and has been declining over a long period, while the tasks of general government have increased in Italy as they have elsewhere; and the current expenditures of central government, the local authorities, various social security institutions and other public or publicly-supported bodies have been boosted by the special factors described in Chapter 3 (i).

While the increase in the budget deficit has provided a welcome support to demand in the recession, it is feared that it will add excessively to inflationary pressures in 1974 when export and investment demand are expected to accelerate. The deficit of 7,700 billion lire in 1973—exceeding by far that of 1972 and the forecast for 1973—is to be reduced to 7,400 billion in 1974, and new expenditures can be authorized only if they are covered by new revenue. This figure has been jointly arrived at by the Ministry of the Budget, the Treasury, and the Bank of Italy. The method used was roughly to calculate, on the basis of estimates of prospective income and savings, the 'financial space' available for the budget deficit which was reconcilable with the financing needs of the productive sector. From estimated savings, the capacity to absorb security issues has been derived. The budget deficit which would develop spontaneously was then estimated on the basis of prospective revenue and expenditure programmes. After allocating to the productive sector that part of available finance required to meet its foreseen expansion, the sustainable non-inflationary budget deficit was arrived at.

Within the expenditure limits set by the over-all figure, it was intended that room should be made for higher public investment. However, given the rigidity of other public expenditure—mainly wages and salaries and transfer payments on which prior commitments have been entered into—budget austerity will once again prevent the desired shift to public investment. This will take up no more than 13 per cent of total expenditure, which is the same share as in 1973.

The lower deficit is to be ensured through reductions in the appropriations of individual Ministries, a curtailment of capital transfers to the endowment fund of public corporations and a cut in the so-called 'global funds' established to meet legislative provisions already approved or to be examined by Parliament. Among the latter, the largest reductions were regrettably made in allocations to the health and school reforms and to funds for the execution of Common Market directives on agricultural programmes. On the other hand, allocations to the Regional Fund for 1974 were raised to more than three times their 1973 level. One major problem to be tackled is the curtailment of public support—amounting to some 4,600 billion lire—to an estimated 59,000 institutions and organs many of which are merely survivors of past decisions, now without useful functions or even without any functions at all.

It is clear that the impossibility of making more room for public investment outlays does not augur well, in the short run, for the various reform programmes and public investment projects which are awaiting implementation. In the somewhat longer run, the possibility of a change in the composition of budget expenditure towards public investment hinges on the authorities' success in putting up more resistance than in the past to pressure from public employees, and in keeping the expenditure of local authorities and various social security institutions and other ones under better control, and on whether strict priorities and appropriate timing can be applied to increases of transfer payments.

On the side of budget revenues it is intended to increase selectively indirect taxation of non-essential goods—and incidentally to reduce luxury consumption—and to raise direct tax revenue through an 'energetic and immediate strengthening of control and assessment intended to hit evasion in the field of social security payments, V.A.T. and direct taxation', all of which the tax reform should facilitate. Economic expansion will itself increase revenues and reduce that part of expenditure which has been connected with the recession. In addition, direct tax rates could be raised and the tax ratio be brought closer to the levels prevailing in other E.E.C. countries.

(iii) LONGER-TERM ISSUES

An official forecast at the end of September 1973 (to be revised and spelt out in more detail in the Annual Plan for 1974 at the end of the year) considered that a 6 per cent rate of GNP expansion in 1974 was possible on the basis of recent demand and output tendencies and the growth of capacities, although specific bottlenecks might develop in some sectors. The O.E.C.D. Economic Survey to be published in December arrives at a more optimistic forecast of real GNP growth of some 7 per cent, on the assumptions that no major strikes will break out, that wage claims and labour cost increases will be comparatively modest and that price increases can be kept within more moderate limits than in the recent past. No account is taken of the repercussions of the oil crisis on prices and the balance of payments. On this basis, residential construction and productive investment are expected to continue their upward path. The realization of the former expectation is dependent on the implementation of administrative provisions as well as, or more than, on cyclical factors, and the latter expectation reflects the need to modernize and rationalize to make up for investment losses of the past. Exports are expected to rise rapidly, despite less dynamic world demand, because of the delayed effects of devaluation; and the contribution of the foreign balance in real terms to GNP growth is foreseen as again substantial, although a deterioration in the terms of trade has to be taken into account in estimating the balance in money terms. Neither balance-of-payments constraints nor strong inflationary pressures are expected to demand over-all policies of restraint.

However, the present situation is much too complex and delicate for a realistic assessment of even short-term prospects to be made on the basis of purely conjunctural forecasts of broad economic aggregates and other traditional economic indicators. Nor can the assumptions about 1974 be turned into reality with the help of short-term economic policy instruments alone, much more effective and differentiated as they may recently have become.

The task which continues to confront the authorities in the short run is to check inflation without inhibiting economic expansion. This is a policy problem which, for varying reasons and in various degrees of intensity and frequency, has been familiar to most advanced industrial countries in the post-war period. In Italy, however, the usual problem of reconciling growth and stabilization or the competing claims on resources of private and social consumption and investment is very much more difficult to resolve than elsewhere. This is in part because economic progress has not been accompanied by social progress, and also because the past pattern of expansion has aggravated structural disequilibria. The simultaneous and pressing demands for a transfer of resources from private to social uses and from the Centre–North to the South of the country as well as for a reduction of the chronic under-employment of the labour potential will have to be met if a resurgence of cost inflation and social unrest—with all their repercussions on prices, the balance of payments, and business confidence—is to be avoided. Moreover, Italy is seriously lagging behind other E.E.C. countries in the modernization and rationalization of its industrial and agricultural structures, and the efficiency of both its public-

and private-enterprise management and its public institutions.

To tackle the short-term problems first and leave action on structural change to a later stage (which appears to be the preference of some policy-makers) might well revive the demand for large wage increases and result in industrial strife, slow down industrial production, set off a new inflationary wave, and in the end call for over-all restrictive measures. Meanwhile a pattern of expansion, unsteered by the public authorities, and allowed to follow the traditional lines of the past, would tend to accentuate further the existing forms of dualism and distortion and to render their elimination even more difficult later on. A concentration of the renewed industrial expansion in the North would involve a continuation of immigration from the South, more congestion and pollution in the Northern industrial centres, with greater shortages of housing and social infra-structures, and thus accentuated competition for public funds between the North and the South. In short, the conjunctural and structural objectives of economic policy have by now become so closely intertwined that to tackle them separately might well mean that neither can be achieved. But to try to solve them simultaneously is an enormous challenge requiring political unity, administrative efficiency, and the support of all economic and social groups.

Italian society thus finds itself at the crossroads. A number of favourable signs seem to point in directions which may lead the economy out of the labyrinth of its difficulties; but the danger of returning to an uneasy and strained development process which would require 'stop and go' policies at frequent intervals and aggravate structural imbalances has not been dispelled.

One major factor which has to be taken into account is the prospective attitude of the trade unions and the outcome of wage negotiations at the plant level. It is true that the three confederations have jointly adopted a policy of moderation in wage claims and demands for changes in working conditions, although they rejected the concept of a 'social truce'.

Instead they now pursue a so-called 'global strategy' which places general economic and social issues in the forefront of their aspirations. They accord first priority to immediate action to raise investment and employment in the South, to create social infra-structures, to enact social reforms, and to improve the conditions of the weaker social groups. Of course, success in checking cost-of-living increases is a primary condition for moderation in wage claims and a co-operative attitude.

Considerable opposition to this course comes from the industrial unions, above all the powerful metal-workers' union, which insist on autonomy with respect to wage claims. The re-opening of wage negotiations at Fiat, which employs some 200,000 workers, is a test case for trade union strategy and for union–employer relations. The national confederations participated in the negotiations side by side with the industrial union, and not only wages and conditions of work but also the broader issues of economic policy, such as investment by Fiat in the South, were discussed. Umberto Agnelli expressed the management's readiness to accept the new approach and to assume the entrepreneurial responsibilities it involves. He submitted concrete plans for new investment projects in the South and for the creation of new jobs. The projects themselves are to be oriented towards products for collective, rather than individual, consumption.

In addition, however, demands for substantial wage increases were submitted. The granting of such increases would certainly add to the difficulties in which Fiat finds itself at the moment, for a number of specific reasons to which the oil crisis has been added. Confindustria considers that more generalized wage concessions of similar dimensions would be excessive, coming as they do on top of the large increases granted in the national wage-round early in the year. It is true that profits have risen substantially since the upturn; but they are beginning, or are likely, to be eroded through the rise in raw-material prices and more recently in oil prices, recent and prospective cost-of-living adjustments, the additional cost burden from higher pensions, child allowances and unemployment benefits, the higher cost of credit and, for the larger enterprises, the price freeze. Another wage explosion or a renewed strike wave would both worsen the investment climate and imperil price stabilization. Whether the trade union confederations maintain the 'global strategy' approach, and whether it prevails over that of the industrial unions and the rank and file, depends on concrete evidence that the authorities as well as the entrepreneurs are ready, and able, to eliminate structural imbalances and to improve the quality of life of the working population. Should such evidence, in the form of positive action, fail to appear in the near future, voluntary wage moderation might well come to an end.

Among the favourable factors which might help the economy to extricate itself from its present difficulties, a change in the political, economic, and social climate can be detected which takes the following forms:

(i) An all-pervading awareness of the danger that Italy might be permanently left behind by the other countries of the European Economic Community;

(ii) The current increase in political cohesion of the government majority and more rapid and determined action on a number of issues, which would have been thought impossible only a short while ago;

(iii) The trade unions have entered the economic scene as responsible and, on certain conditions, co-operative partners of the Government in shaping the economic future of the country;

(iv) Leading industrialists have become more conscious of the new role they could and should perform, in active co-operation with the other social partners, in joint planning.

So far specific action to change the economic and social environment has been taken or is concretely contemplated by the authorities in a number of fields. The reform of the budget structure and the preparation of a medium-term budget stand out as a key measure, which will also help to limit the past abuses of the public administration. The tax reform is another positive step in this context, although the fight against tax evasion is still to come. The regions, which have been called upon to assume a number of important functions within the government machinery, have now been supplied with more adequate funds; and, although the total amount allocated to them is still rather modest, it is sufficient in the light of what the regions are ready to spend at the moment.

As to the action in the South, several important improvements in policies and institutional arrangements are being made or foreseen. (c.f. p. 131 ff. for previous arrangements.) Cassa funds are to be greatly increased and the complicated procedures for obtaining subsidized credit, involving the Ministry for the South, the Interministerial Committee for Economic Planning, and credit institutions, are to be shortened and simplified. Steps have been taken to clear the jungle of incentives granted in other areas, which has grown and spread through political and group-interest pressures. It was erroneously believed in the past that, by increasing the discretionary power of public authorities, more headway would be made with publicly planned investment in the South. Instead this resulted in much abuse and waste. In a new scheme, objective criteria and automatic procedures are being introduced, and the creation of new jobs is to be the main objective. Concerning the system of 'special projects', efforts are being made to link and co-ordinate investment programmes, but action has to remain pragmatic in the absence of an administrative system which is geared to programming. Finally, there are the first signs of an acceptance by entrepreneurs of the so-called 'development contracts' for investment in the South, although resistance comes from the rank and file workers. They fear that they may be compelled to forgo certain concessions, in terms of wage increases and the improvement of working conditions, in exchange for increases of investment and employment in the South.

Emphasis is also being placed on the promotion of industrial programmes. Priority is now being given to a long-term plan for the oil industry which had been elaborated already before the outbreak of the oil crisis. It aimed at increasing government control over the sector and ensuring national supplies at reasonable prices. Specific action is also being taken to increase national production and to rationalize imports in the meat and animal husbandry sector, whose difficulties have been largely responsible for the growing food deficit and high consumer prices.

In the social field, the Interministerial Committee for Economic Planning has presented an interim plan for housing. (See Chapter 8.) To break through the deadlock over the Housing Reform, 300,000 dwellings are to be built in three years as a result of a simplification of procedures, and a concentration of funds from the budget and from the institution which collects workers' contributions for social housing.

But many negative factors continue to complicate the tasks of the authorities. In the short run, no lessening can be expected of the difficulties arising at the operational level from political fragmentation, the pressure of vested interests, and the inefficiency and obstructionism of the public administration. To this set of problems is added the difficulty of reconciling all-out budgetary austerity with development policies and social reforms.

Another critical issue at present is the deterioration of the balance of payments—due, this time, to a large current account deficit. The consistent current account surpluses in the past were a reflection of an under-utilization of resources at home at the same time as expansion had to be checked because of the large deficits incurred on capital account. At present, and leaving aside the exceptional recent developments which contributed towards raising the trade deficit, a current deficit may well be considered as normal for a relatively poor country approaching the full employment of its resources, particularly after a prolonged period of investment stagnation. But policies must be adjusted to this new situation. Until conditions for investment at home become more attractive than they have been in the past, the measures already in operation to check capital exports will remain necessary and could well be supplemented by action to stimulate inflows of foreign capital. Special efforts might be made to promote foreign investments in the South, though their success would inevitably depend in part on the success of the general development policies for the region. Now, at the end of 1973, the oil crisis is superimposed on all the existing problems as a new and serious threat to the level of production and employment and to the efforts to check the rate of inflation and to reduce the balance of payments deficit. Even if oil supplies turn out to have been less sharply curtailed than was originally feared, the steep rise in oil prices is likely to have a particularly severe impact on the Italian economy, tending to intensify an already large current account deficit and an exceptionally high rate of inflation. Italy's dependence on energy imports is greater than that of any other Western European industrial country; and the motor-car industry and connected industrial activities play a key role in output, employment, and exports.

It is not expected that, under these circumstances, price increases can be slowed down from their exceptionally rapid 1973 rate. But another key problem is the impact on the balance of payments of an estimated additional import cost of some $4·5 billion. Other oil-importing countries face similar problems and the drastic change in the distribution of international currencies and in the relative strength of individual currencies will have to be tackled by new international agreements on currency arrangements, the financing of deficits and on the supply of industrial exports to the oil-producing countries. Within this new international framework, Italy's previous policy of financing deficits through bank borrowing will be reinforced and efforts will be made to reduce the food deficit and to find new export outlets.

In these circumstances, and in addition to immediate measures to reduce oil consumption, the policy course so far adopted by the Italian authorities is to make up for the short-fall of output and employment and private-sector demand, likely to arise from the depressing impact of a sharp increase in expenditure on imports and from other effects of the crisis, through the adoption of a so-called 'new model of development'. A shift of resources from private to public transport and, more generally, from private to collective consumption and investment is to be brought about. It has been pointed out repeatedly in the past that such a change is highly desirable *per se*; but it may be doubted whether it is feasible to carry through a massive re-deployment of resources sufficiently rapidly and effectively to offset much of the effect of the oil crisis in the near future. Moreover, serious disagreements have arisen once again within the government on the choice of policy instruments for combatting the crisis.

(iv) ITALY AND THE COMMON MARKET

There have been very few references so far in this study to the economic effects of Italy's adherence to the European Economic Community. The main reason is that an attempt at a comprehensive assessment of the impact on the Italian economy, and on the actions of the Italian authorities, of the opportunities provided and the constraints imposed by membership of the Community would require a study as large as this has already become. To disentangle the effects of membership from those of other influences is difficult, and many of the likely longer-run effects—like the longer-run future of the Community itself—are particularly difficult to foresee. However, some brief general assessment of the effects of membership must obviously be attempted.

Integration with the European Community has clearly conferred substantial benefits upon the Italian economy, but it has also created a number of difficulties and constraints. The conflict between adherence to E.E.C. rules and the pursuit of domestic development objectives has probably been more acute, and has probably been more frequently obvious, in Italy than in most other member countries because the Italian economy is burdened with the weight of its regional problems and of its partial underdevelopment in other respects also. But some of the benefits which might have been derived from E.E.C. membership did not materialize because of the failure of the Italian authorities to implement some E.E.C. directives.

The benefits obtainable from trade integration and the rapid expansion of intra-Community trade—in terms of income, output, and productivity growth—are evident in a country which is highly dependent on imports of raw material, food, and energy. For reasons stated in Chapter 1 (ii), Italian export industries were in a particularly favourable position for some time to profit from trade integration. But the export-led pattern of expansion brought in its wake an accentuation of regional, sectoral, and social imbalances which have not been corrected by counteracting measures (see section (iii) in Chapter 1).

The Community's progress towards financial integration has placed a number of constraints on domestic economic policies, especially since it was not accompanied by a simultaneous co-ordination and harmonization of such policies among member countries. The freedom of international capital movements was reflected, in the special Italian economic and political climate of recent years, in massive capital outflows, in part to benefit from more favourable fiscal and interest rate conditions in other countries and in the Eurodollar market and in part for purely speculative reasons. To protect a vulnerable balance of payments and to reconstitute international reserves, the authorities felt compelled, in conditions of fixed exchange rates, to adopt restrictive or cautious monetary policies which frequently ran counter to domestic policy objectives. But in the currency crisis of 1973, they chose to resume their freedom of manoeuvre by abandoning the Community rules on a common exchange rate policy and floating the lira (see Chapter 4).

The gradual adjustment of Italian wage levels to those prevailing in other E.E.C. countries has also created difficulties, because of the persistence of large divergences in productivity between regions, sectors, and enterprises, though how far membership of the Community hastened this process of adjustment must remain in some doubt.

It was in the agricultural sector that the most thorny problems arose, from a confrontation of the Common Agricultural Policy with the special conditions of poor resources and agricultural backwardness in many areas of Italy. While the large outflow of labour from agriculture has raised the productivity of those remaining and has contributed towards increasing agricultural incomes, it had an adverse effect on the age and skill composition of agricultural employment. Furthermore, the reduction of the labour force in agriculture was not accompanied by a consolidation and amalgamation of farms or by a better adaptation of soil utilization to natural endowment and to changes in the pattern of demand. Nor was sufficient action taken to improve professional skills and education, to create collective infra-structures, social services, and alternative employment opportunities on the spot. Small farm-size and fragmentation continued to prevail and not enough was done to develop new forms of co-operation and marketing, the latter continuing to be controlled by parasitic forms of intermediation. The substantial financial means allocated to agricultural transformation have only been partially used, and large unspent appropriations have accumulated at the Ministry of Agriculture. As a result of these and other policy omissions and delays, which affect the agricultural sector as they do all other sectors dependent on public action, agricultural targets for 1966–70 were not achieved, agricultural investment slowed down in the latter part of the 1960s, and the food deficit has substantially increased in recent years.

Italian agriculture has thus not profited much from E.E.C. aid to the structural transformation of the sector; and the provisions of E.E.C. agricultural price policies have operated to Italy's disadvantage. A complex system of combining protection against agricultural imports from non-member countries with subsidization to permit the liquidation in such markets, at competitive prices, of high-cost excess production did not favour Italian agriculture. In the first place, Italy is a large food-importer and does not dispose of substantial surpluses of products requiring subsidy to make them exportable. Secondly, and in highly schematic and simplified terms, the common price-support policies worked in the following way: under powerful pressures from some other E.E.C. countries, high protection against imports from non-member countries was mostly granted to those commodities which the former produce—such as cereals, milk and dairy products, and meat—but for which Italy is highly import-dependent. On the other hand, low duties on extra-E.E.C. imports were set on typical Mediterranean products—such as oleoginous products, tobacco, fruit and vegetables—to enable the processing industries in other E.E.C. countries to obtain low-cost imports, although special subsidies were granted to Italian producers on a case to case basis. In very general terms, the outcome was that Italy could not avail itself of low world-market prices for some of its large imports while it obtained low Community preference for some of its own export products. Strong protection stimulated autarkic tendencies generally, and in Italy encouraged the expansion of cultures with a low labour-intensity such as cereals, and retarded the planned shift to intensive branches of production. The share of fruit and vegetables in agricultural production, which was intended to be raised during the First Plan period, in fact declined.

Italy's position in the European Agricultural Guidance and Guarantee Fund reflects these anomalies. Italy, with a weak agricultural sector, ran large deficits in the Guarantee section of the Fund and thus contributed substantially to financing the surpluses accumulated by France and the Netherlands, both of these being countries with strong agriculture. The surpluses Italy built up in the Guidance section of the Fund are a reflection of the failure of the Italian authorities to make full use of E.E.C. finance for agricultural development projects.

A large part of the responsibility for not benefiting more fully from membership in the E.E.C. rests with the Italian authorities themselves. Successive governments did not have a clear and continuous view of the objectives they wanted to attain through integration, and Italian representatives could therefore not make a sufficiently forceful and coherent case for Italy's specific problems and needs. While Italian delegates participated actively, and often very constructively, in E.E.C. deliberations, the decisions and directives elaborated at the Community level—some of which were of the greatest importance to the country—were often approved with great delays and not followed up and put into operation at home. For instance E.E.C. contributions to structural transformations in agriculture or to regional development schemes have often not been fully or immediately utilized because the projects concerned were not fully prepared or completed or because funds to finance the required national contribution were not made available.

One striking example of failure to adhere to E.E.C. commitments was the introduction of the value-added tax only on 1 January 1973—that is, three years after a deadline which had been accepted without much ado. The fact that Italy holds the record for the number of its infringements of the E.E.C. Treaty and subsequent regulations, although many Italian representatives and international civil servants enjoy a deservedly high reputation for their efforts for integration, is once again an illustration of the political and administrative obstacles to efficient policy-making.

It seems hardly worthwhile at this stage to speculate on the prospects for changes in the objectives, rules, and mechanisms of the European Economic Community, the role Italy might play in bringing them about, or the benefits it might derive from them. One of the major tests of Italy's ability to participate in and benefit from the economic and social development of the Community will be the common regional policy and the use to which an enlarged Regional Development Fund will be put. Italy's benefits from the Fund—whatever its size or the criteria applied for its allocation—will partly depend, once again, on the timely submission of well-prepared projects. But, as with regional development incentives provided from national sources, the supply of E.E.C. finance will not be sufficient, by itself, to halt and eventually to reverse the strong tendencies for a concentration of expansion in the already industrialized areas. An E.E.C. policy for industrial location and planned and balanced regional development is required if Italy's South is not to be pushed into a still more peripheral position by advancing European integration; and if this were to happen the consequences for Italy as a whole could be disastrous.

NOTES

CHAPTER 1: THE MAIN PHASES OF DEVELOPMENT

1. This analysis draws largely upon the following annual or biannual publications: Ministero del Bilancio e della Programmazione Economica, *Relazione Generale*; Bank of Italy, *Relazione Annuale*; ISCO (Istituto per la Congiuntura), *Rapporto al Consiglio Nazionale dell'Economia e del Lavoro*; O.E.C.D., *Economic Surveys, Italy*; U.N. Economic Commission for Europe, *Economic Surveys and Economic Bulletins*. See also A. Graziani (ed.), *L'economia italiana: 1945–1970*, Il Mulino, Bologna, 1972.

2. G. Fuà, *Notes on Italian Economic Growth, 1861–1964*, Giuffré, Milan, 1966.

3. E. F. Denison, *Why Growth Rates Differ*, Brookings Institution, Washington, D.C., 1967.

4. A. Graziani, op. cit.; G. Fuà and P. Sylos-Labini, *Idee per la programmazione economica*, Laterza, Bari, 1963; G. Fuà, *Notes on Italian Economic Growth*; V. Lutz, *Italy, a Study in Economic Development*, Oxford University Press, London, 1962; F. Forte, *La Congiuntura in Italia, 1961–1965*, Etas Kompass, Milan, 1966.

5. See A. Graziani, op. cit.

6. For a partly theoretical discussion of the interplay of factors influencing private investment, see P. Sylos-Labini, 'Prices, Distribution and Investment in Italy, 1951–1966: an Interpretation', *Banca Nazionale del Lavoro*, no. 83 (December 1967).

7. See A. Graziani, 'Dall'espansione alla depressione', and C. Napoleoni, 'Le inefficienze causano la crisi', in A. Graziani (ed.), *L'economia italiana: 1945–1970*, Il Mulino, Bologna, 1972.

CHAPTER 2: THE RECENT DEVELOPMENT CRISIS

1. O.E.C.D., *Monetary Policy in Italy*, Paris, 1973.

2. U. La Malfa, former leader of the Republican Party and Minister of the Treasury in the new Centro-Sinistra Government.

3. In *Considerazioni Finali*, Annual Report of the Bank of Italy for 1972 published on 30 May 1973.

4. See G. Ruffolo, Appendix to 'Rapporto sull'Esperienza di Programmazione'.

5. See ISCO, *Rapporto al Consiglio Nazionale dell'Economia e del Lavoro*, 31 October 1972.

6. G. Ruffolo, op. cit.

7. Bank of Italy, *Relazione Annuale* (1970).

8. G. Ruffolo, op. cit.

9. See in particular the Annual Report of October 1972 of IFI (Industrial Finance Institute) of which Mr. Giovanni Agnelli is President.

CHAPTER 3: BUDGETARY AND MONETARY POLICY

1. In addition to the annual Italian and international reports quoted in Chapter 1, note 1, the major sources used for this section were: B. Hansen, *Fiscal Policy in Seven Countries, 1955–1965*, O.E.C.D., Paris, 1968; O.E.C.D., *Fiscal Policy for a Balanced Economy*, Paris, 1968; G. Ruffolo, 'Rapporto sull'Esperienza di Programmazione', Rome, 1973; and L. Izzo, A. Pedone, L. Spaventa, and F. Volpi, *Il controlo dell'economia nel breve periodo*, F. Angeli, Milan, 1970.

2. See *Revenue Statistics of O.E.C.D. Member Countries 1968–1970*, O.E.C.D.

3. See F. Forte, *Strategia delle riforme*, Etas Kompass, Milan, 1968.

4. G. Ruffolo, op. cit.

5. See L. Izzo *et al.*, op. cit.

6. G. Ruffolo, op. cit.

7. See Ministero del Bilancio, Appendix to the *Relazione Generale*; 1971 and 1972.

8. G. Ruffolo, op. cit.

9. See ISCO, *Rapporto del gruppo di studio sui problemi di analisi economica e di politica economica a breve termine*, Rome, 1969.

10. See N. Andreatta, 'La politica congiunturale e le strutture monetarie e creditizie', Perugia, 1972.

11. See P. Sylos-Labini, 'La politica monetaria resta deflazionista', in *L'Economia italiana: 1945–1970*, Il Mulino, Bologna, 1972.

12. G. Carli, in 'Considerazioni finali', Bank of Italy, *Relazione Annuale* (1972).

13. O.E.C.D., op. cit.

CHAPTER 4: THE BALANCE OF PAYMENTS AND THE LIRA

1. See F. Masera, economic adviser to the Bank of Italy, 'Autonomous Capital Movements: The Italian Experience in the Past Decade', in *Die Restriktionen im internationalen Zahlungsverkehr wichtiger Industriestaaten*, Schulthess Verlag, Zürich, 1973.

2. F. Masera, op. cit.

3. See A. Graziani, in *Il Mondo*, 5 July 1973.

CHAPTER 5: THE LABOUR MARKET

1. See O.E.C.D., *Economic Surveys, Italy*, 1972; G. Ruffolo, Appendix to 'Rapporto sull'Esperienza di Programmazione'; *Relazione Generale*, 1971; G. La Malfa and S. Vinci, 'Il Saggio di Partecipazione della forza di lavoro in Italia', *L'Industria*, no. 4 (1970); M. de Cecco, *Una interpretazione Ricardiana della dinamica della forza di lavoro in Italia nel decennio 1959–1969*, Siena, 1972; CENSIS, *VI Rapporto sulla situazione sociale del paese*, October 1972.

2. See F. Caffe, 'Considerazioni sul Problema della Disoccupazione in Italia', *Rivista internazionale di scienze economo de commerciali*, CEDAN, Padua, 1973.

CHAPTER 6: REGIONAL DUALISM: THE SOUTH

1. A. Graziani (ed.), *L'economia italiana: 1945–1970*, Il Mulino, Bologna, 1972.

2. A. Graziani, op. cit.

3. A. Graziani, op. cit.

4. A. Giolitti, *Riforme e Sviluppo*, report delivered to the Convegno Nazionale del Partito Socialista, Rome, 17–19 May 1973.

CHAPTER 7: PUBLIC CORPORATIONS

1. For an excellent study of the theory and practice of state entrepreneurship in Italy see S. Holland *et al.*, *The State as Entrepreneur. New Dimensions for Public Enterprise: the IRI State Shareholding Formula*, Weidenfeld and Nicolson, London, 1972. For a condensed survey containing useful statistical information, see O.E.C.D., *Economic Surveys, Italy*, Paris, 1972.

2. S. Holland *et al.*, *The State as Entrepreneur.*

3. The data are derived from O.E.C.D. elaborations of national statistics published in 'Basic Data on Public Corporations', O.E.C.D., *Economic Surveys, Italy*, Paris, 1972.

4. Ministero delle Partecipazioni Statali, *Relazione Programmatica*, First Volume, Rome, 1973.

5. A. Giolitti, in an interview with the *Espresso*, 13 January 1973.

6. G. Carli in Bank of Italy, *Relazione Annuale*, 1972.

7. Bank of Italy, *Relazione Annuale*, 1972.

8. G. Carli in Bank of Italy, *Relazione Annuale*, 1972.

CHAPTER 8: STRUCTURAL REFORMS

1. A. Graziani, op. cit.

2. G. Ruffolo, op. cit.

3. G. Ruffolo, op. cit.

4. P. Sylos-Labini, 'Sviluppo Economico e Classi Sociali in Italia', *Quaderni di Sociologia*, no. 4 (1972).

5. G. Ruffolo, op. cit.

6. G. Ruffolo, op. cit.

CHAPTER 9: ECONOMIC PLANNING

1. G. Ruffolo, op. cit.

2. See O.E.C.D., *Economic Surveys, Italy*, Paris, 1972.

READING LIST

PERIODIC PUBLICATIONS

INTERNATIONAL

Economic Commission for Europe, United Nations, *Economic Survey of Europe* (Geneva).

O.E.C.D., *Economic Outlook* (Paris).

O.E.C.D., *Economic Surveys, Italy* (Paris).

ITALIAN

Bank of Italy, *Relazione Annuale* (Rome).

Cassa per il Mezzogiorno, *Relazione e bilancio* (Naples).

Istituto Nazionale per lo Studio della Congiuntura (ISCO), *Rapporto al Consiglio Nazionale dell'Economia e del Lavoro* (Rome).

Ministero del Bilancio e della Programmazione Economica, *Relazione Generale* (Rome).

Daily newspapers: *Il Coriere della Sera*; *La Stampa*.

Periodicals: *L'Espresso*; *Il Mondo*; *Il Mondo Economico*.

GENERAL WORKS

ALLEN, K. J., and MACLENNAN, M. C., *Regional Problems and Policies in Italy and France* (Allen and Unwin, London, 1970).

ANDREATTA, N., 'La politica congiunturale e le strutture monetarie e creditizie' (Perugia, 1972).

BAFFI, P., *Studi sulla moneta* (Giuffré, Milan, 1965).

BALLONI, V. (ed.), *Lezioni sulla politica economica in Italia* (Edizioni di Communità, Milan, 1972).

BASSEVI, G. (ed.), *La bilancia dei pagamenti* (Il Mulino, Bologna, 1971).

BELLONE, G., *Il dibattito sulla moneta* (Il Mulino, Bologna, 1972).

CAFFE, F., 'Considerazioni sul Problema della Disoccupazione in Italia', *Rivista internazionale di scienze economico de commerciali* (CEDAN, Padua, 1973).

CENSIS, *VI Rapporto sulla situazione sociale del paese* (Rome, 1972).

DE CECCO, M., 'Economic Policy in the Reconstruction Period, 1945–51', in S. Woolf (ed.), *The Re-birth of Italy* (Longmans, London, 1972).

—— *Un interpretazione Ricardiana della dinamica della forza di lavoro in Italia nel decennio 1959–1969* (Siena, 1972).

DENISON, E. F., *Why Growth Rates Differ* (Brookings Institution, Washington, D.C., 1967).

FONDAZIONE EINAUDI, *Nord e Sud nella società e nell'economia italiana di oggi* (Turin, 1968).

ꓳRTE, F., *La Congiuntura in Italia, 1961–65* (Etas Kompass, Milan, 1966).
—— *La Strategia delle riforme* (Etas Kompass, Milan, 1968).
FUA, G., *Notes on Italian Economic Growth, 1861–1964* (Giuffré, Milan, 1966).
—— (ed.), *Lo sviluppo economico italiano* (F. Angeli, Milan, 1969).
—— and SYLOS-LABINI, P., *Idee per la programmazione economica* (Laterza, Bari, 1963).
GIOLITTI, A., *Riforme e Sviluppo* (Convegno Nazionale del Partito Socialista, Rome, May 1973).
GRAZIANI, A., *et al.*, *Lo sviluppo di un'economia aperta* (E.S.I., Naples, 1969).
GRAZIANI, A. (ed.), *L'economia italiana: 1945–1970* (Il Mulino, Bologna, 1972).
HANSEN, B., *Fiscal Policy in Seven Countries, 1955–65* (O.E.C.D., Paris, 1968).
HOLLAND, S., *et al.*, *The State as Entrepreneur, New Dimensions for Public Enterprise: The IRI State Shareholding Formula* (Weidenfeld and Nicolson, London, 1972).
Istituto Nazionale per lo Studio della Congiuntura (ISCO), *Rapporto del gruppo di studio sui problemi di analisi economica e di politica economica a breve termine* (Rome, 1969).
Istituto per la Riconstruzione Industriale (IRI), *Esercizio* (1971–2).
—— *Notizie* (June and September 1972).
IZZO, L., PEDONE, A., SPAVENTA, L., and VOLPI, F., *Il controllo dell'economia nel breve periodo* (F. Angeli, Milan, 1970).
JUCKER, N., *Italy* (Thames and Hudson, London, 1970).
LA MALFA, G., and VINCI, S., 'Il saggio di partecipazione della forza di lavoro in Italia', *L'Industria*, no. 4 (1970).
LUTZ, V., *Italy, A Study in Economic Development* (Oxford University Press, London, 1962).
MACK-SMITH, D., *Storia d'Italia dal 1861 al 1969* (Laterza, Bari, 1969).
MASERA, R., 'Autonomous Capital Movements: The Italian Experience in the Past Decade', in *Die Restriktionen im internationalen Zahlungsverkehr wichtiger Industriestaaten* (Schulthess Verlag, Zürich, 1973).
Ministero del Bilancio e della Programmazione Economica, *Progetto di Programma di Sviluppo Economico per il Quinquennio 1966–70* (Rome, 1965).
—— *Progetto 80, Rapporto Preliminare al Programma Economico Nazionale, 1971–75* (Rome, 1969).
—— *Documento Programmatico Preliminare, Elementi per L'impostazione del Programma Economico Nazionale, 1971–1975* (Rome, 1971).
—— *Relazione Previsionale e Programmatica per L'Anno 1973* (Rome, 1972).
—— *Programma Economico Nazionale, 1971–1975* (Rome, 1972).
—— *Programmazione* (Periodical).
Ministero delle Partecipazioni Statali, *Relazione Programmatica* (Rome).
NOBECOURT, J., *L'Italie à vif* (Éditions du Seuil, Paris, 1970).

O.E.C.D., *Fiscal Policy for a Balanced Economy* (Paris, 1968).
—— *Monetary Policy in Italy* (Paris, 1973).
OLIVI, B., *Da un'Europa all'altra* (Etas Kompass, Milan, 1973).
PEDONE, A., *La politica fiscale* (Il Mulino, Bologna, 1972).
PETRILLI, G., *L'État entrepreneur* (Robert Lafont, Paris, 1971).
POSNER, M. V., and WOOLF, S. J., *Italian Public Enterprise* (Duckworth, London, 1967).
PRODI, R., *Sistema Industriale e Sviluppo Economico in Italia* (Il Mulino, Bologna, 1973).
RUFFOLO, G., 'Rapporto sull'Esperienza di Programmazione' (Rome, 1973).
SARACENO, P., *Risultati e Nuovi Obbietivi dell'Intervento Straordinario* (SVIMEZ, Rome, 1970).
—— *Il Mezzogiorno tra Congiuntura e Riforme* (SVIMEZ, Rome, 1972).
SVIMEZ, *Il Mezzogiorno nelle Ricerche della SVIMEZ 1947–1967* (Giuffré, Rome, 1968).
—— *Gli investimenti industriali agevolati nel Mezzogiorno, 1951–1968* (Giuffré, Rome, 1971).
SYLOS-LABINI, P., 'Prices, Distribution and Investment in Italy, 1951–66: an Interpretation', *Banca Nazionale del Lavoro*, no. 83 (December 1967).
—— 'Aspetti dello sviluppo economico italiano', in *Problemi dello sviluppo economico* (Laterza, Bari, 1970).
—— *Sindicati, inflazione e productività* (Laterza, Bari, 1972).
—— 'Sviluppo Economico e Classi Sociali in Italia', *Quaderni di Sociologia*, no. 4 (1972).

INDEX